CAPE BRETON MEMORIES
Margaree & Beyond

JOEL S. SCHWARTZ

Flint Hills Publishing

Cover Design by Amy Albright

stonypointgraphics.weebly.com

/Flint Hills Publishing
Topeka, Kansas
Tucson, Arizona
www.flinthillspublishing.com

Printed in the U.S.A.

Paperback Book ISBN:
978-1-966323-45-7

Electronic Book ISBN:
978-1-966323-46-4

Library of Congress Control Number 2025923390

DEDICATION

Dedicated to the memory of my loving parents,
Hannah and George Schwartz,

and in memory of my devoted wife,
Rhoda Schwartz,
who helped me discover and rediscover Cape Breton.

Preface

C*ape Breton Memories* is a labor of love. I have wanted to write about the summers my family and I spent in this corner of Nova Scotia for quite some time. The Margaree Valley and environs is a special place, one which we have visited over many summers. This book is a departure from the type of writing I have engaged in the past.

Previously, I have written extensively about 19th century natural historians such as Charles Darwin, Thomas Henry Huxley, Alfred Russel Wallace, Robert Brown, and others, and how their voyages and explorations influenced the development of the theory of evolution. Thus, writing about personal reminiscences is a new and challenging experience.

I have incorporated numerous photographs that my Dad and I took over the years when we vacationed in Nova Scotia. As a naturalist, he took numerous photographs during his field studies in the parks and woodlands of New York City and vicinity, as well as Connecticut and the Berkshires. Plant and animal life were his main subjects of interest, but he took many family photographs and landscapes of the places we visited as well.

My interest in photography largely was stimulated by the vacations we enjoyed in Cape Breton, initially with a simple box camera that was my mom's, and then a Brownie Reflex Synchro Model manufactured by Eastman Kodak. My dad encouraged my taking photographs, and my mom assisted me as well.

Dad's collection of 35mm. transparencies and prints, in addition to the prints that I took as a young boy, are a part of the photographic record of our holidays in Cape Breton. I have also included the photos I took as an adult, supplemented by my wife Rhoda's Polaroid pictures, some taken by our sons, Mark and George, and a few that my sister took of our fishing for salmon and trout in the waters of the Margaree when we helped her and husband, Dr. Robert Davidson, celebrate their 40th wedding anniversary in Cape Breton. These photographs reinforce the memories we have of this magical place, Margaree.

Swampscott, Massachusetts 2025

The Margaree Valley, near the Tompkins Farm,
Margaree Ford in August 1948.

Introduction

Cape Breton Island, a part of the Canadian province of Nova Scotia, is a place of picturesque scenery, friendly people, and many interesting and notable summer residents. The fresh and clean air has made it an ideal place to paint, write, think, and enjoy fishing in the waters of the Margaree River. The Island's outstanding attributes make it well worth the distance one must travel to get there.

In the years immediately after the end of World War II, Cape Breton Island was not an unknown destination for U.S. residents, but its distance from population centers like New York City discouraged U.S. travelers from undertaking the trip. However, for artists and writers from the New York area, weary of the crowds and the pricey scene on Cape Cod,

3

summer plans became more adventurous. Those who had the time and inclination began to journey to this special place in the northeastern corner of Nova Scotia.

Why did my family travel over a thousand miles by automobile to spend several magical summers in this wonderful corner of the world? My parents had a friend, an artist who studied with the American painter and illustrator, Frank Vincent DuMond at the Arts Students League in New York. DuMond was a regular visitor to Cape Breton in the early years of the twentieth century, and he painted fishing scenes as well as the people and landscapes of the Margaree River Valley. Before the Second World War, DuMond sometimes brought his art students to the area, including my parents' friend and her husband. They spent their summer holidays on a farm in the Margaree Valley in Cape Breton, and they convinced my parents that they, too, should visit Cape Breton. Thus, art and friends led my family to discover this remarkable place for themselves.

My earliest impression of Cape Breton was the first morning after I arrived at night as a seven-year-old boy, accompanying my parents and my sister. I realized I was on a working farm, filled with animals that I had previously only read about in books: cows, horses, pigs, and chickens. There were three barns that workers were filling with hay, and other workers were busy performing numerous tasks. There the scent of the gathered hay was omnipresent. The Margaree River was near the farmhouse and barns, and although it was quite early in the morning, there were men fishing in the waters of the river. The picturesque farm scene was something I had not previously experienced first-hand. In addition to the beautiful green pastures surrounding the farm, there were other fields filled with oats that had an off-white appearance.

The Travel Film, "Cape Breton Island"

One Saturday morning recently, the Turner Classic Movie Channel broadcast a travel short entitled "Cape Breton Island." The piece was filmed in 1948, the very summer I first went to Cape Breton. Although the travelogue was edited down to nine minutes in length, I looked forward to the prospect of viewing an early color film that would capture the essence of the island that I remembered from my boyhood. Perhaps what was transmitted through the lens of the camera would affirm what I remembered from my childhood and family photographs.

The film was produced by the film studio, Metro Goldwyn Mayer (MGM), one of many such travelogues that were shown in movie theaters to accompany feature films years ago. It began at the Alexander Graham Bell Estate near Baddeck, a relatively prosperous town with a Scottish flavor. Baddeck (pronounced with two syllables: Buh-deck) is inland, with the Gulf of St. Lawrence to the west and the Atlantic Ocean to the east. During the summer of 1948, visitors were welcomed to tour the grounds of the Bell estate and enjoy its view of Lake Bras d'Or (pronounced: Brah-door), a large tidal estuary of the Atlantic Ocean. Today, tourists are no longer allowed on the grounds of the Bell estate, Beinn Bhreagh (pronounced: Ben Vree-a). However, there is the excellent Bell Museum in the town of Baddeck, and many of Bell's inventions are preserved there, including the planes he designed. During the summer months, summer visitors and year-round residents sail on Lake Bras d'Or, browse the stores in Baddeck, and take in the region's beauty.

After showing Baddeck, there was a depiction of the Margaree Valley, a more pastoral region, the locale I was most anxious to see. There were glimpses of farms nestled along the

Margaree River as it flowed snake-like on its way to Margaree Harbour and the Gulf of St. Lawrence. I looked forward with great anticipation to see images that I first observed as a seven year old who traveled to the Margaree Valley. The narration in the film confirmed that, in addition to the people who come to the Margaree to fish, the picturesque region attracted artists who found the scenery irresistible.

What made this such a powerful experience for me was that this brief travelogue was produced at the very time my family visited Cape Breton in August 1948. There were vivid scenes of the abundant oat fields in the Margaree Valley, and of farmers busily harvesting hay in preparation for winter, storing sufficient food for their livestock. The film reinforced my first glimpses of a part of the world containing some of the best features of Irish and Scottish landscapes, with a bit of the Berkshires and the Hudson River Valley in New York State thrown in for good measure.

The descendants of Acadians who settled in Cape Breton were also prominently featured. The Acadians are French-speaking people who settled and still live in the region predominately north of the Margaree Valley. These descendants live in the vicinity of the village of Cheticamp, where, until recently, some had continued to fish commercially in the Gulf of St. Lawrence. For many years, there were colorful fishing vessels tied up at the docks in Cheticamp, but that way of life has faded. A scene vividly showed a woman and her daughter at their looms, busily weaving the hooked rugs that local artisans produce. It accurately captured what I recalled during my first encounter with life in this region of Cape Breton. This activity was a successful Cape Breton craft industry that continues to this day.

The film showed the system of ferries that connected

different regions of Cape Breton Island to each other and to the Nova Scotia mainland. Those ferries have been replaced since my initial visit in 1948. A causeway was built between Auld Cove on the mainland and Port Hastings on the Island connecting Cape Breton with the rest of Nova Scotia. Additionally, bridges have replaced the local ferries that help bind different regions of Cape Breton together. But outwardly, Cape Breton today remains in many ways the same as in 1948, although many of the farms no longer play as central a role in the region's economy. The roads have now been paved and many of the farmhouses dating back to the nineteenth century have been replaced by more prosaic structures, similar to tract houses in suburbia.

The film concluded with a few glimpses of Sydney, the port city located on the eastern end of Cape Breton on the North Atlantic coast. Sydney was once the primary industrial city in Nova Scotia. It was a coal-mining center and had a steel mill in the vicinity as well. It was sometimes called the "Pittsburgh" of Nova Scotia, but that term is no longer applicable, because now the heavy industry is long gone.

Today, Sydney is a destination for cruise ships, with its harbor and vistas that allow one to view the island's brilliant fall colors. The city is near the restored fortress of Louisbourg, now a mecca for visitors, with its reconstructed buildings depicting life in the 18th century. The area was the scene of significant battles during the French and Indian War (The Seven Years War), during the time in which Britain gained control of this region as well as the rest of Canada. The war ended 13 years before the American Revolution began. The French and Indian War was not mentioned at all in this travel piece, because when it was produced in 1948, the fortress was in ruins and clearly was not the tourist attraction that it is today.

After viewing this travelogue, I decided to share my own memories of Cape Breton from my childhood and through my adulthood, to the present. There is much to relate, for Cape Breton has a rich history including many gifted and unusual people. It remains a very special place for me and my family.

What Makes Cape Breton So Special

The island's scenery is wondrous, but not in the way places like the Grand Canyon, Bryce, and Zion are. It has a subtler beauty of lush greens with winding roads that bear some resemblance to the coastal highway of California. However, Cape Breton has a greener and a gentler landscape than the coastal region of California. If you travel in a clockwise route around Cape Breton Highlands National Park, you will journey from the waters of the Gulf of St. Lawrence to that of the Atlantic Ocean within just a few minutes.

The scenic vistas in the Cape Breton Highlands National Park stand in contrast to the picturesque pastures of the farms that still dot the Margaree Valley. The Valley is filled with beautiful views, imbued with various shades of colors, but particularly green. The farms stand nearby the Margaree River as it winds its way through the Valley.

But scenery is not all that the island offers. The year-round inhabitants also make visits to Cape Breton worthwhile. Cape Bretoners as a group are friendly. When I went to Margaree with my parents after the conclusion of World War II, the only music one heard was the tunes played on bagpipes at the Gaelic Mòd. This has changed. In recent years, there has been a renaissance of "Cape Breton Music," an amalgam of Scottish, Irish, and Acadian tunes. This exciting development has taken place over the course of the past 35 to 40 years. Fiddlers and other musicians have made Cape Breton a home for music lovers. Many people had feared that this music might die out but now it has become more widely known due to this cultural renaissance.

A lack of local opportunities for the better-educated offspring of large farm families remains an ongoing problem because of the demographic changes that have taken place in Nova Scotia. Many talented young people reluctantly head west to Ontario and Canada's western provinces for suitable employment commensurate with their training and education. Although farming has diminished in importance during the postwar years, new opportunities have emerged that have provided more diversified employment. More native-born Cape Bretoners are now able to find work without leaving their beloved island, with tourism a major driving force generating employment opportunities. The Cape Breton I remember from boyhood has changed, but the beautiful countryside and wonderful people remain and make this a very special place.

The Tompkins Farm, Margaree Ford, August 1948.
Taken from the West Bank of the Margaree River.

Chapter One
Our Family's Adventure

I looked forward to summer vacation and the end of the school year. On Wednesday, June 30, 1948, the last day of school finally arrived. I had just completed the second grade in Mrs. Adele Towne's class at P.S. 120 in Queens, New York. Although I enjoyed the second grade and most of the first grade with Mrs. Towne, it seemed as if the school year would never end. I walked home with my kid sister Susan, who was finishing kindergarten. My mother, Hannah Schwartz, greeted us outside. I was a bit puzzled. I thought that there must be a reason why she was waiting for us. Her faint smile suggested to me that she had some good news to report and was eager to share it with us. She told us that after my father, George, finished his summer teaching at New York University in July, we would be going to Nova Scotia for our August vacation. This news piqued my interest. I did not realize—how could I? I was seven and a half years old then—that this trip would play a significant role in my life.

Why did my parents drive for nearly four days and travel almost 1,100 miles with two young children to make this journey? It was the happy result of my parents' friendship with Lou and Hannah Cohen who discovered Margaree in the late 1930s. Hannah Cohen (née Moscon), was an artist who studied with Frank DuMond at the Arts Students League in Manhattan. DuMond told his students about Cape Breton, specifically about the Margaree Valley. The students asked if they could continue their classes during the summer in Margaree at their own expense. Thus, Hannah Cohen was part of a select group who accompanied DuMond on his vacations in Cape Breton in the late 1930s. After the end of World War II, Hannah Cohen and her husband, Lou, traveled with their young daughter, Beatrice, on their own to Cape Breton, specifically the Margaree Valley. They told my parents about Margaree, and in 1948, my parents decided that it would be an unusual and exciting adventure to vacation in Cape Breton.

Lou Cohen was a pioneer in the profession of court stenography. He enjoyed extensive vacation time during the summer months, which was quite a contrast to his early life. Lou grew up poor on the Lower East Side and had to quit school in the second grade, but he was determined to educate himself. He was well-versed in many different subjects and had artistic talent, especially in the art of sculpture. Through this and his visits to Cape Breton, Lou became quite proficient in the craft of Acadian woodcarving.

Our Adventure Begins

In early August 1948, we left our home in Queensborough Hill in the family—car a gray, pre-War Oldsmobile sedan that my parents had purchased earlier that year. My parents anticipated a three-and-a-half to four-day journey. We drove over the Whitestone Bridge onto two-lane highways into Connecticut, which was still rustic and underdeveloped in the immediate post-War period. I was able to look out on bucolic Connecticut scenes from the car window because the New England Thruway did not exist back then. As we rode on the Wilbur Cross Parkway, I remember the strong scent of tobacco that emanated from farms growing the leaves that were made into cigar wrappers. Initially, I sat between my parents in the front seat. I remember I did not want to relinquish this privilege, watching my mother turn the pages of the triptych as we progressed northeast on our journey. My sister Susan and I fought for that front seat position for the duration of our journey.

As we motored steadily northeast through Connecticut, I enjoyed the comfort of the car and the scenery that rushed by the window. Connecticut farms were often divided by stone walls, remnants of colonial times. On this first trip to Cape Breton, we rode past Boston, which appeared then as a somewhat tired but large New England town. I observed that New England and maritime Canadian towns and cities had their street signs on the sides of their buildings.

We headed to New Hampshire, and our route took us deep into the White Mountains. Even as a seven year old, I was struck by the beauty that surrounded us. After traveling all day, my father told us that we had covered over 365 miles. That first night we stayed in a bright, white cabin in the picturesque valley town of Twin Mountain, New Hampshire.

The second day we crossed into Maine where the roads seemed narrower. We were unable to quite match the previous day's journey, covering only 320 miles. We stayed overnight in cabins outside of Ellsworth, Maine. When my father asked the proprietor whether there would be heat in the morning, he was informed that heat would be provided. At six o'clock in the morning, there was a loud thud on the porch of the cabin. A cord of wood was tossed there, and that was our heat.

We did not linger longer that chilly August morning. After breakfast, we were on the road again. The cabins are still visible today when traveling on Route 1 through the Down-East region of Maine, but they are no longer pearly white. They are painted in brilliant pastels, each one bearing a different bright color. Those cabins have survived the age of motels, superhighways, and jet travel, and they have become the subject of strikingly colorful photographs.

On this third day, we crossed from Calais, Maine into St. Stephen, New Brunswick, Canada. My mother remarked how friendly the people were in Canada, waving to passing cars in contrast to the staid dour faces we had encountered earlier in Maine. We soon stopped in Saint John, New Brunswick, an interesting Loyalist city. Here, my father purchased a Harris Tweed jacket and a Hudson Bay shirt from the Manchester Robertson Allison and Scoville Brothers (Oak Hall) department stores, two wonderful emporia on Saint John's King Street. Unfortunately, all such stores are now gone, in the process of urban decline and renewal that began more than forty years ago. Malls and shopping centers pushed these stores into oblivion.

We stayed that third night in cabins situated on the Nova Scotia mainland near the Northumberland Strait, overlooking the Gulf of St. Lawrence. The air seemed fresh and light in the summer maritime air, regardless of the weather conditions. Those cabins still exist, having been modernized and converted into housekeeping units, suitable for longer tourist stays. My father estimated that we would to arrive in Cape Breton before dark the next day.

Cape Breton

Cape Breton is a large, mitten-shaped island that lies to the northeast of the Nova Scotia mainland. In 1948, there was no causeway that would allow one to easily drive onto the island as is possible today. My family took a small ferry at Mulgrave onto the Nova Scotia mainland and crossed into Cape Breton at Port Hawksbury. We traveled north on the western shore of the island, with the Gulf of St. Lawrence on our left and then headed a bit inland. At Judique, the paved highway became a pitted dirt road. To our dismay, we got a flat tire on the road, and it was Sunday as well. But we soon learned that the flat would not be much of a problem. There was no end to the friendly Cape Bretoners who stopped, eager to assist my father in changing the tire. The difficult part of the task was removing our luggage from the trunk to get to the spare. The friendliness of Cape Bretoners was reinforced time and again during our month-long stay.

The delay meant that we arrived in the Margaree Valley toward dusk and my father had to call the Cohens, who came to direct us from Margaree Forks to Margaree Ford, the postal address of the farm where we were to stay. The proprietress of the farm was also the postmistress at Margaree Ford (later renamed Fordview). The location received its name because it was located where the horse-drawn hay wagons forded the

Margaree River. It remains to this day the most picturesque location in the Margaree Valley.

Susan and I had a comfortable room with soft beds and warm quilts. We slept very well that night, and in the morning, I went out to explore our new surroundings in the daylight. The locale was wondrous to someone who grew up in urban Queens, New York City. The farm actually consisted of two adjoining farms and included a chicken coop, three barns, cows, horses, and pigs. Farmhands were busy filling the barns with hay in preparation for the winter months. My favorite animal was a dapple-gray horse who did not have to perform heavy work such as pulling plows. The farms were not mechanized then, except for a tractor which I would sit on, pretending I was driving our family car.

Rose Tompkins, in front of her home in
Margaree Ford, August 1948.

Rose Tompkins was the proprietress of the farmhouse where we stayed. Her brother, Mike Tompkins, owned the adjoining farm. Because Mike already had a growing family who lived at his farmhouse, he had no room for guests. Rose, unmarried, had plenty of room and had welcomed guests for years. This was before the Nova Scotia tourist office promoted farm vacations in a formal program designed to aid tourism. Rose, a highly independent woman, instituted her own farm-holiday stays, and we quickly learned at breakfast that she often hosted prominent writers and artists such as Frank DuMond. They came for the scenery, for rest, and for fishing in the Margaree River.

Over the years, other young musicians, writers, and artists have come to Cape Breton Island. The young artists who stayed in Margaree were not wealthy by any standard, and Ms. Tompkins's charges were a bargain even then. She billed my parents only four dollars a day for all of us, two adults and two children, including three meals a day. Years after our initial stay in Cape Breton, my sister and I each returned to Margaree on our respective honeymoons.

After our honeymoon, my wife Rhoda and I did not travel to Margaree for a number of years. There were many good memories there, and many people who were an integral part of this experience were no longer alive. I thought it would be better to put those wonderful memories aside. But after our two young sons were born, we began again to take vacations in Cape Breton. We took our sons, Mark and George, to Margaree, and developed a renewed love for the verdant hills and fields and have developed fresh experiences with new friends in Margaree. My visits to this special place live on in my memory. How fortunate I was to have spent time there during my childhood!

Marcel Tabuteau

Sitting across from us that first morning at breakfast in Rose's dining room was Marcel Tabuteau, a pre-eminent classical oboist, and his wife, Louise. Tabuteau spent forty years as the principal oboist with the Philadelphia Orchestra. He trained many musicians even after his retirement from the orchestra and from the Curtis Institute of Music, which he had headed. Tabuteau had a profound influence on the musical world because many of the world's prominent oboists he taught trained the next generation of oboists. However, Tabuteau did not come to Margaree to play the oboe; he visited every summer to fish for salmon in the Margaree River. When he caught a good-sized salmon in the morning, Rose would prepare it for lunch for all the guests who were staying there.

Tabuteau stayed the entire summer that year, as he had for many years. 1948 would prove to be the last year he would travel to Margaree to spend his vacation time, except for a brief visit years later. The next summer (1949), he went to Prades, France, near the Spanish border, to participate in the annual Pablo Casals Festival. He continued to travel to Prades and Perpignan to play with many illustrious musicians including Isaac Stern, Alexander Schneider, Rudolf Serkin, Eugene Istomin, and John Wummer.

Tabuteau briefly returned to Cape Breton one last time, in the early 1960s, for a last look before retiring to his native France. Whenever I hear the recording of Tabuteau playing Johann Sebastian Bach's Concerto for Oboe and Violin (BMV 1060)—with Casals conducting the Prades Festival Orchestra and Isaac Stern playing the violin—I recall my family's experience meeting with Tabuteau and how lucky we were to get to know him.

Marcel Tabuteau, with Susan (Schwartz) Davidson and
Joel Schwartz, on his acreage near Whale Cove, August 1948.

Marcel Tabuteau with his salmon, at Rose Tompkins' farm,
Margaree Ford, August 1948.

[**Note 1**:] We were the last family on our block to own a car. My parents had to sell the family car, a Ford, at the outbreak of World War II, not because of gasoline rationing, but because of the scarcity of rubber for tires. In the early 1940s, we lived in a garden apartment in Kew Gardens, Queens and did not own our own home. People who owned private homes were able to store their late 1930s Chevys, Pontiacs, or other prewar cars in their garages. They put their cars on cinder blocks, drained the fluids, detached the battery, and waited out the war. When the war ended in 1945, rubber tires became plentiful again. The well-built cars from the late 1930s sprouted up all over the neighborhood in Queensborough Hill, like mushrooms after rain. Because we had moved into our semi-attached house in early 1944, we did not enjoy the luxury that our neighbors had. My mother sometimes spoke wistfully about the Ford my parents had to sell before the war. When my father bought our Oldsmobile in late 1947, my mother immediately named it "Nelly," and "Nelly" faithfully took us on many trips over the next three years. But the first trip to Nova Scotia was the most memorable.

[**Note 2:**], I recently read about the graphic novelist, Kate Beaton in *The Sunday Boston Globe*. Her initial work, "Reading Dickens in the Oil Fields of Alberta," describes her experience in Alberta and the pollution she encountered there. Many of her subsequent works reflect her interest in preserving the environment. Eventually, she returned to her beloved home in Mabou, Cape Breton, a picturesque area south of the

Margaree Valley. After graduating from Mount Allison University in New Brunswick, she did not wish to become a teacher. She headed to western Canada, and her experiences there led her to write several graphic novels. Her work has won several prizes, and she has written for the *New Yorker*. Eventually, when she returned to Mabou, her homecoming exemplified the hold this special place has on serious artists and people of letters.

Chapter Two:
Margaree Ford: Life on Rose and Mike Tompkins's Farm

Before visiting Cape Breton, the animals I encountered in my life were not farm animals, but those I had observed at the Bronx Zoo, a frequent excursion for my family in the 1940s. My parents were longtime members of the New York Zoological Society and were very much interested in supporting the zoo. My father was a naturalist and had always been a keen observer of nature. My mother's artistic sensitivities widened my own appreciation for the beauty in the natural world, although she did not have the opportunity to develop her talent because of the depression in the 1930s. She worked to help support our family, backing Dad's work, caring for Susan and me, and running our home. She spent considerable time and energy taking us to music lessons and pottery classes in Manhattan, trips that involved long bus and subway rides.

The first summer I spent in Margaree in 1948 was a revelation for my family and me. Our stay on a working farm was quite different from anything I had previously experienced. When I returned to Margaree in 1963 after a 13-year hiatus, the thing that struck me most was the familiar scent of freshly-gathered hay coming from the pastures and barns. It triggered a rush of emotion and brought back memories of many summers before, when I was a young boy discovering an exciting new world.

When I woke up that first morning in Rose Tompkins'

farmhouse, I got dressed quietly and went down to the two barns where Rose kept her animals and the stored hay which would feed them during the long winter months. I frequently visited the farm animals that Rose kept in her barns and pastures, particularly the horses, the cows, and the pigs. The horses were the chief attraction for me. They were used extensively for many tasks on the farm, especially plowing and pulling the hay wagons. The horses were also a means of transportation. Rose did not own a car; after all, few people did at that time. She had a horse-drawn buggy which she took on Sundays to St. Michaels church in the village of Margaree (now called East Margaree). On several occasions, particularly during inclement weather, my father drove Rose to church.

"Dapple Gray," near the Margaree Ford School, August 1950.

One of the horses particularly fascinated me; a dapple-gray horse that stayed in the barn most of the day. I called this horse, "Dapple Gray." The horse seemed to be pleased with my attention. When I gathered up enough courage, I fed him some of the loose pieces of hay I collected from the floor of the barn by hand. I was puzzled why my favorite horse was excused from heavy work. Perhaps it was too old, although it did not seem so to me at the time. When we returned to Margaree in 1950, "Dapple Gray" was no longer in the barn in a small pasture adjoining the one room schoolhouse on the property, the Margaree Ford School. I never discovered the reason why the horse enjoyed privileged treatment, (and why it was no longer kept in the barn) in spite of my persistent questions

I enjoyed visiting the pigs that Rose kept in an enclosure in the barn. They remained close to one another and communicated with their grunts and snorts. A door from this space led to an outside, fenced-in area that served as a sty. When I went to see the pigs in the barn, I found them friendly. Rose allowed Susan to bring food to the pigs, and when they caught sight of her, they would rush from the sty and eagerly assemble into their place in the barn to receive the food.

The dairy cows took up most of the space in the barns when they were not grazing in the pasture. Rose maintained an organized schedule for the care and milking of these animals. I often went down to Rose's kitchen at six in the morning to watch her employ a machine that separated the cream from the milk. Milking took place twice a day, at dawn and then about four in the afternoon. I generally did not watch the cows being milked because the chore was conducted before I arose. Rose did her own milking by hand, and was sometimes assisted by the people she employed to perform this chore because Nova Scotia dairy farmers did not use milking machines in the 1940s. I learned years later from my mom that Rose took the additional precaution of pasteurizing the milk, heeding my mother's request to do so, although Rose assured my mother that her cows were regularly tested and were free of disease.

Pigs on Tompkins Farm, August 1948.

There was a chicken coop next to the barns and Rose had many chickens who ran around during the day and roosted in the coop at night. Several times, I accompanied Rose when she collected the eggs produced overnight. I was not too fond of the fowl although I liked most birds. One day, near Mike Tompkins's barn, a rooster that I was trying to befriend nipped at me. Everyone else found that funny but I was not amused. I learned that day that sometimes it was wise to give space to even these somewhat-domesticated animals.

I did not grasp, or perhaps did not want to know, the eventual fate of these animals. As far as I knew, the cows were just for milking and were not slaughtered for meat. The chickens were there to produce eggs and also did not imagine that they too could be sacrificed. I did not think of that latter possibility back then, or perhaps did not want to know, similar to my attitude regarding the pigs who I thought were sort of pets who did not do very much except eat and amuse guests. Those animals were my friends, and my parents protected us from the harsh realities of life for the most part. Rationing had ended only a few years before, so my young mind did not make much connection with the occasional roast beef dinner treat we enjoyed and the animals I befriended.

The author in his favorite spot, August 1948.

I spent some of my time sitting on a tractor that was located near Rose's home, close to the bottom of the hill nearby. I pretended I was behind the wheel of my father's Olds, driving to Cape Breton. I discovered that when I applied some pressure on the clutch petal on the tractor, the tractor vibrated slightly, giving me the sensation of movement. Because the tractor was turned off, it seemed fairly safe, but I never mentioned the full extent of what I was doing on the tractor. I was thankful it continued to operate smoothly without any malfunction, performing the tasks it was intended to do, and relieved that I would not be scolded for this bit of mischief.

Rose and Mike allowed us to wander about and experience a bit of farm life. Despite their busy schedule running their farm, they allowed us to sit atop the hay wagons when they

25

forded the Margaree River. On one occasion, Mike let my sister and me take the reins of the plow horses.

Susan and the author with Mike Tompkins in Margaree Ford, August 1950.

Susan with Mike Tompkins on his farm in Margaree Ford, August 1950.

The author and Susan atop hay wagon, fording the Margaree River, August 1950.

My parents loved their summers in Margaree as much as Susan and me. Tabuteau was interested in their company, particularly Dad's knowledge as a naturalist and Mom's appreciation and understanding of art and music. After dinner one evening, he invited all of us to his 100-acre plot of land near Whale Cove, near where we sometimes swam. From his property we had an excellent observation point for viewing the Gulf of St. Lawrence. My father took pictures of the sunset from that point. I was fascinated by the numerous sheep grazing on the rocky terrain; Tabuteau had allowed a neighboring farmer to have his sheep graze there.

Tabuteau professionally had the reputation of a demanding taskmaster, but when he vacationed in Cape Breton, he was patient and understanding. I learned about this first-hand. I discovered that Rose's bathroom scale could be adjusted to any desired weight. In those years, I was rather thin and wanted to be heavier to feel more grown up. I discovered that I could register additional weight on the scale if I set the scale beyond zero. Unfortunately, on several occasions, I failed to readjust the scale to zero. At breakfast or lunch one day, Tabuteau said that he was concerned that his weight was fluctuating and thought he should go to a doctor. I had to confess to my adjusting the scale. I probably did so either to my mother or more likely blurted out my confession at the time. My father was a trifle annoyed with me. However, Tabuteau seemed amused, probably relieved that his fluctuation in weight did not stem from a health problem but rather the foolish prank of a seven-year-old.

Marcel Tabuteau on his Whale Cove acres, August 1948.

My sister and I were young enough to share the large attic bedroom. My bed was near the door. It was cozy, with a warm quilt. My sister's bed was located under the eaves. A cord attached to the room's light ran parallel to the ceiling, and dipped down near my bed. The cord was within easy reach so when my sister gave me permission, I was able to pull the cord, thereby shutting off the light.

Before retiring for the night, my mother came in to read to us and say goodnight. The first summer (1948), she read *Alice in Wonderland* from my copy of Lewis Carroll's classic work with John Tenniel's fabulous illustrations. Years later, when I spent time in Oxford, England, particularly during summer afternoons, I recalled my mother's reading about a young person's childhood in Victorian England, remembering my own summer idyll in Cape Breton.

Hannah Schwartz in Margaree Ford, August 1948.

That first summer we stayed in Margaree Ford was the most rewarding for all of us. Because we occupied two bedrooms in Rose's farmhouse, and the Tabuteaus shared the other guest bedroom, the Cohens graciously stayed at the Duck Cove Inn in Margaree Harbour during our stay in August 1948. The original Duck Cove Inn was an old Victorian wooden structure that was well maintained by the owner, Jean LeBlanc.

He had little patience for a curious seven-year-old boy so when I started to handle the croquet set located on a rack on the side of the building, he scolded me in no uncertain terms. When we met the Cohens at the Duck Cove Inn on future visits, I made certain that I stayed clear of Monsieur LeBlanc, just as I avoided the rooster.

George Schwartz in Margaree Ford, August 1948.

In 1950, when we returned for our vacation in Cape Breton after the horrendous polio epidemic of 1949, I observed a side of my mother I was previously unaware of. As we pulled into Rose's farm in Margaree Ford that first week of August, Mom became filled with unbridled joy, but at the same time, she grew quite emotional. Through tears of joy, she pointed out the familiar sites of our wonderful summer two years before, pointing to the trees and other landmarks she recognized from her memory of our previous summer in Margaree. I realized then how much this place meant to her.

Chapter Three
My Delayed Return to Cape Breton

Traveling to Cape Breton, first as a child of seven and then as a nine-year old, was an opportunity to leave Queens, the then semi-urban borough of New York City. I was able to experience a very different world. Although Cape Breton was in another country, there was no language barrier. Because the people were kindhearted, we felt quite at home.

These were not the only delights Cape Breton afforded us. From a practical standpoint, Cape Breton Island had little ragweed. My parents thought that I would get relief from my late summer allergy woes. Our stay at Rose Tompkins's farm in the Margaree Valley was inexpensive in those early postwar years. My parents thought that having a number of delightful beaches nearby was also an advantage when traveling with young children.

In spite of all our positive experiences and the advantages of taking our summer holiday in Cape Breton, we did not go back as a family. During the decade after we visited Margaree in 1950, certain circumstances prevented our return to Cape Breton. My parents, who felt that Susan and I would benefit from some sort of "camping" experience, sent us to summer camp where we would learn to swim and play with children our own age. To afford this, my parents took jobs in "toney camps" in the Pocono mountains, in Pennsylvania, where we were campers. At the time, these were comfortable and expensive camps. My father was the "nature counselor" in the boys' camp and my mother taught arts and crafts in the girls' camp. Dad's efforts included the development of a "nature trail." The nature program was invigorated by his efforts, resulting in new experiences for the campers. Sadly, the majority of the campers showed little interest in this activity. The camp directors were also largely indifferent to Dad's efforts. Sports were the primary activities, and other things were of secondary importance. However, both Susan and I learned how to swim when we were campers.

Later in the decade, I had various camping jobs. For several years I washed dishes in the kitchen of a camp for underprivileged children in western New Jersey. Later, I was a counselor at a day camp in Roslyn, Long Island. Between my freshman and sophomore years at college, I worked as an assistant to the renowned Columbia University geneticist, Theodosius Dobzhansky, helping to collect Drosophila (fruit flies), preparing jars of food for the colonies of flies, washing the discarded jars, and making slides of the giant salivary gland chromosomes of Drosophila. The flies were collected near Yosemite Park, in Mather, California, and were the subjects of cytological examinations at the American Museum of Natural History's laboratory in southeastern Arizona. Quite an opportunity for an 18-year-old!

Despite these varied summer experiences, we all yearned to return to Cape Breton. When Mom passed away in the spring of 1960 after a long illness, Dad promised that we would revisit Margaree, in part as a tribute to Mom's memory. But the three of us never returned together as a family because Dad received an opportunity to develop teaching programs at the New York Botanical Garden. Susan and I spent the summer of 1960, several months after Mom's death, immersed in summer courses at NYU while my father worked at the New York Botanical Garden. I also had a summer job working in a biology laboratory at NYU, receiving a tuition break for my work. My father thought our studies would take our minds away from the enormous loss we had suffered. Thus, our returning to Cape Breton would again be deferred.

In August 1963, I took a camping trip to Cape Breton with Susan's fiancé, Robert Davidson. We camped out in New Brunswick and Nova Scotia. When we arrived in Margaree Ford after thirteen years, I noticed that the roads had changed. They were now paved, and the path of the road that previously cut through Rose and Mike Tompkins's farm now went around the barns. Eventually, the remnants of the dirt road that had basically bisected the farm deteriorated over the years so the landscape was somewhat altered. The beautiful hill behind Rose's house had been carved out in the building of the road, thanks to the Nova Scotia Highways Department. Mom and Dad had sometimes sat on that hill in the late morning or afternoon so I knew they would be disappointed if they saw what happened to one of their favorite spots.

After thirteen years, Rose was obviously older but did not seem very much changed. She remembered my family and me. Robert and I stayed a day or two on the farm. It was more mechanized and guests stayed a shorter time than they had thirteen years before. Rose still served meals. I felt a certain amount of sadness that I could not share this experience with my parents, but I was glad to be back in Margaree. Robert informed Rose that he and Susan wanted to return the next summer to spend their honeymoon there.

Susan and Robert did spend their honeymoon at Rose's Farm in Margaree in June 1964. Luckily for them, this was the last year Rose would be accepting guests. She was going to retire and turn over the farm to her nephew, Alec Miller, and his family. Alec took part of her porch and added more space to Rose's sewing room to create private quarters for her to live in during her retirement. She no longer had to walk upstairs as frequently as she had done before. Rose did not get to enjoy this arrangement for long. She passed away in 1965.

However, Alec was happy to rent out this little nook, and Rhoda and I spent our honeymoon there in August of 1966, sans meals. We had a small refrigerator and a stove, so we were able to have breakfast and occasionally lunch there. Because the roads were now paved, we had more mobility than my parents had enjoyed, enabling us to find suitable places to eat dinner in the area's inns and restaurants.

Rhoda found the farm experience new—certainly different from her urban upbringing in Brooklyn—and she took to the animals there as I had as a young boy. It was lucky for us that Alec was still willing to rent out the space. He never liked farming and hired local people to do some of the farm work until his children were old enough to work the farm. He then worked full-time at the local Credit Union in the village of Margaree (East Margaree). We were very glad that he could accommodate us and staying at Rose's place still meant a great deal to me.

Rhoda in foreground behind Rose's barn, August 1966.

Rhoda at Rose Tompkins-Alec Miller's Farm, August 1966.

Rhoda seated on thresher, August 1966.

Chapter Four
The Beaches of Margaree

Oone of the most pleasurable experiences my family and I enjoyed during the summers we spent in Cape Breton was the visits to the beaches in the Margaree Valley. The Margaree River flows gently toward the Gulf of St. Lawrence. In Margaree Harbour, the river enters the Gulf, close to Laurence's General Store and is adjacent to an attractive beach.

Margaree Harbour Beach is a nicely situated swimming area on the Gulf of St. Lawrence less than a quarter of a mile in width. When I revisited Margaree as an adult, I observed it was busier than the other more secluded beaches in the area. I also observed that the majority of the local people and tourists generally went there during the warm summer months when they did not want to drive to the less accessible beaches located in the area. In terms of charm and view, it is picturesque enough, with its view of Belle Côte, a small, Acadian fishing village situated across the inlet from Margaree Harbour.

The waters in the Gulf are warm, which is true of most of the beaches in the Canadian Maritime Provinces (with the exception of the Bay of Fundy in the western region of New Brunswick). There is a geological explanation for this phenomenon. Unlike the waters off the coast of Maine, the Gulf of St. Lawrence waters are relatively shallow. In Maine, the shoreline is rocky and it drops off precipitously; the water quickly becomes deep and cold. One cannot wade out for any distance before starting to shiver. In Margaree, as well as

Prince Edward Island, for example—a region also known for its picturesque beaches—one can wade a considerable distance with the waters remaining relatively shallow. A fortunate consequence is the relative mildness of the water temperature. There is no abrupt jolt to the body's system when you enter the water, as is the case in Maine and the Bay of Fundy.

My father enjoyed the excursions to the beach because the water was shallow and warm. There was a paradox to his enjoyment of the Cape Breton beaches that I discovered years later; he could not swim. The warmth and the shallowness of the Gulf allowed him to wade out into the refreshing waters. My mother, a strong swimmer, went into the water briefly, and spent her time either reading—Ross Lockridge's *Raintree County* one summer, William O. Douglas's *Of Men and Mountains* another summer—or talking with their friends, the Cohens. However, our trips to the beach were primarily for Susan's and my benefit.

We spent many pleasant hours in the waters of the Gulf. I also enjoyed looking for shells and egg cases of skates, a boneless cartilaginous fish related to sharks and stingrays. Eventually my parents, upon the recommendation of other intrepid summer residents, ventured further. We drove southward to the more secluded beaches. These beaches were even more picturesque swimming areas.

The first of these was Whale Cove, a beach approximately the size of the one in Margaree Harbour. When we drove there, my father was able to park his car on a hill overlooking the beach. Across the road were the 100 acres owned by Marcel Tabuteau. We had become familiar with the setting of Whale Cove Beach before we swam there because early in August 1948, my family had accompanied Tabuteau and his wife to their property. There we enjoyed the sunsets from the hills overlooking the Gulf. To my knowledge, neither Tabuteau nor his wife swam at Whale Cove Beach or any of the other beaches in the area. My father took pictures of the sun setting. The scene seemed almost magical as the sun slipped into the Gulf.

This was one of Tabuteau's final opportunities to view these majestic sunsets and enjoy the peace and quiet of this rustic setting. When Tabuteau was selected to be one of the world-class musicians to perform at the Pablo Casals Festival in Prades and Perpignan, France the following summers (an event that grew in importance in the 1950s), it was the capstone of his illustrious career. Tabuteau, who was aging and near retirement from his position at the Philadelphia Orchestra, sensed he would not return to Cape Breton. Before we returned home that summer, he made my parents an unusual offer. Because he and his wife liked my parents very much and enjoyed their company, (and tolerated my sister and me), he offered his 100 acres of land to my parents. My parents were moved by his generous offer but did not accept it because they did not have the means to take care of his property.

Subsequently, the land was sold and developed. In later years, when we drove down the road on the way to the beach at Whale Cove or further, we observed how popular the beach had become. The new owner of Tabuteau's acres had cabins constructed and aligned in monotonous, parallel rows there. The area became a mecca for families with children who wished to take advantage of a rustic setting where they would be within walking distance of the Whale Cove Beach. The "population explosion" in Whale Cove unfortunately resulted in its losing some of its charm.

Susan (Schwartz) Davidson at Whale Cove Beach, August 1950.

The author as a seven-year-old at Whale Cove Beach.

Knowledgeable people knew that the best beach was a bit further down Shore Road, as the road wound its way south along the shores of the Gulf of St. Lawrence. Chimney Corner was a large and relatively unoccupied beach, at least during the summers of 1948-50. Chimney Corner Beach was near a vintage one-room schoolhouse. A local sheep farmer, named Evans, owned the land on and around the beach and welcomed anyone who wanted to swim there, free of charge.

Chimney Corner Beach is a truly majestic setting, with large imposing cliffs which dominate the landscape and are covered with abundant greenery. It is worth the extra few miles of driving, including the quarter mile that one must drive on an easy-to-miss dirt road to reach the beach. When I went with my parents, we saw few people at Chimney Corner Beach. My father recalled that you could change into your swimming trunks right on the beach, or at least the children did. Even so, my mother ensured that our modesty was protected by strategically employing beach towels and blankets.

After the time I traveled with my parents, local townsfolk and visitors swam there with greater frequency and enjoyed this quiet refuge. When the Nova Scotia government completed the construction of a causeway in 1955, connecting Cape Breton Island to the Nova Scotia mainland, the beaches became busier. Road-building efforts made what were previously-remote Cape Breton locales, more accessible.

In later years, when Rhoda and I vacationed in Cape Breton, we changed into our swimming gear at the Normaway Inn where we were staying because, by that time, more people had "discovered" Chimney Corner Beach. This wonderful beach had become busier, but the reward remained the same. Evans was a hospitable but inconspicuous host. As the volume of people increased in time, he removed some of the large stones on a small hill overlooking the beach, thereby allowing visitors to park more easily. We observed the license plates of cars from different provinces in Canada as well as some from the "States," a term Canadians use when referring to America.

Over the years, I have continued to enjoy this stretch of sand, often walking the quarter-mile length of Chimney Corner Beach by myself, looking for signs of marine life, and reflecting on the wonderful memories the beach evokes. In recent years, the beach has furnished few of these objects, probably due to the increasing number of people visiting and the more serious environmental degradation afflicting our planet. But the memories of the land and the friendly people remain.

Hannah Schwartz with Susan and author,
Chimney Corner Beach, August 1950.

The waters are delightful and refreshing, warm enough to forget the shock of entering the very cold northern waters found elsewhere. When our sons were young and traveling with us, my wife Rhoda enjoyed some of the same delights I enjoyed as a boy, although she disliked certain aspects of the beach despite being a good swimmer. She recalled the crowded beaches in Brooklyn where she grew up. Her father dragged Rhoda and her mother, both fair-skinned and redheaded, to those busy places where they baked in the hot sun for hours.

Rhoda, during visits to the beaches in later years as our boys grew older, preferred to sit on a beach towel, sometimes without changing into her bathing suit. After an hour or so, she started looking at her watch and reminded our boys and me that it would soon be time to leave. She enjoyed the scenery and the fresh air but did not enjoy herself at the beach as much as the rest of us. This contrasts with our honeymoon (August 1966) when she seemed to enjoy the beaches of Margaree a bit more and seemed to be happier with her appearance in a bathing suit.

Rhoda Schwartz at Chimney Corner Beach, August 1966.

The Beaches of Margaree add to the loveliness of the locale, as places that blend with the surroundings and add to the rich experience of summer vacations in this corner of Canada. They are picturesque places to swim—places where the sand literally sparkles and where the waters offer striking blue, and at times, greenish-blue hues. The beaches, with clean, light-colored sand, and surrounded by beautiful hills covered by plentiful greenery, are delightful. Although more people have flocked to the Gulf of St. Lawrence coastline in recent years, the "beaches" could still be considered semi-private, at least compared with the urban beaches that I have grown familiar with. They are quiet, so one can be at peace.

The author with Mark and George,
Chimney Corner Beach, early 1980s.

Rhoda at Chimney Corner Beach, summer 1986.

Mark and George enjoying the waters at
Chimney Corner Beach, early 1980s.

Rhoda, Mark, and George at Chimney Corner Beach, early 1980s.

Mark and George enjoying the sand at
Chimney Corner, early 1980s.

Chapter Five
Berry Picking and Jam

I have vivid memories of picking blueberries and raspberries during our vacations in Cape Breton. It was an integral part of the time spent in Margaree. Lou Cohen led everyone in this pursuit. He knew the best locations in the Margaree Valley for the berries. To be candid, as a preteen boy I regarded this activity as more of a chore at the time, a task I thought was tedious and not altogether very interesting. However, my parents enjoyed it, and Susan fell in with all the participants, save me.

The raspberry bushes seemed to grow best alongside the dirt roads and near the banks of the Margaree River. I disliked picking raspberries, although I always enjoyed eating them. They were difficult to pick; their red juice-stained clothing and the berries often crumbled as they were picked. Additionally, it was quite buggy near the raspberry bushes, with black flies in great abundance. I sometimes begged to get out of this activity, preferring to play with a toy car or find some other divertissement.

The blueberries were a different matter. Picking them was easier, true for both the low bush and high bush varieties. They grew in somewhat drier areas. These bluish orbs did not crumble in your hands when picked and were not as juicy. They came off the bush quite easily. I grew quite adept at picking them, almost in an effort to compensate for my indolence as far as the raspberries were concerned. It was also less buggy near the blueberry bushes, and one could accomplish a great deal in a relatively short amount of time.

The Cohen's daughter, Beatrice, told me that in July, there were plentiful strawberries found in the region, and they were not as difficult to pick as the raspberries. Many years later, during the summers when Rhoda, Mark, George, and I visited Margaree, we sometimes traveled to Margaree earlier in the summer, in July. But on those occasions, we did not find many strawberries to pick. I also noticed during the years we vacationed in August, there were less raspberries available. So perhaps there were other factors at play. The summers had become warmer, and the road construction over the years may have altered the habitat as far as the raspberries were concerned. Not so with the blueberries; they continue to be found in abundance.

Lou and my dad consolidated the berries in Mason jars that Lou and Dad had purchased in the general stores in the area. During our first summer in Margaree, in 1948, we often gave the berries to Rose, who would incorporate them into the meals we had, serving them as plain desserts or in pies. In 1950, during our second vacation in Margaree, we did much more berry picking and many more Mason jars were filled. *What would become of all this booty?* I wondered at the time. At the end of our stay, my question was answered. The evening before our departure, in early September, everyone was gathered in Rose's kitchen. Lou was using Rose's stove, cooking the berries and treating them in a special way. I soon realized he was making jam out of the collection from the entire summer. As a result of his labor, there were many jars filled with strawberry, raspberry, or blueberry jam. I vividly remember Lou carrying the jam jars to a storage area beneath the floor in Rose's kitchen.

Lou Cohen picking Highbush blueberries in August 1948.

All the while, the radio blared out news of military clashes in Korea, something no one seemed to be prepared for. Another war, not long after the terrible one that had ended just a few years earlier. All this meant a great deal more to me once we returned home and I began fifth grade. It represented a significant marker in time; the 1950s had begun and somehow the more innocent post-war world I had known seemed to have changed. I was also older, and people seemed to me more cynical.

My parents packed many jars of the jam in our car on our journey home, "fruit" of our labor from our holiday. Lou threw in a few jars of strawberry jam from the berries he and his family had picked earlier in the summer, prior to our arrival. My parents stored the jars of jam in my mother's sewing closet in the finished basement in our home in Queensborough Hill, (a part of Flushing, Queens, NYC). The jam lasted for years, a constant reminder of the joy and satisfaction we all experienced from the summers we spent in Margaree. My parents particularly enjoyed the jam during the 1950s, keeping alive the memory of such wonderful summers spent in Cape Breton, as sadly, Mom and Dad were never able to return.

When Rhoda and I were on our honeymoon in 1966, we did some berry picking. We enjoyed both the raspberries and blueberries as dessert. Rhoda liked picking the berries because she had never engaged in this sort of activity prior to traveling to Cape Breton.

We returned to Margaree in 1974 when Mark was a year-and a-half old. We were joined by our friend, Martin Hutner who was with us for the first leg of our trip. Martin was a good friend whom I met when I was engaged to Rhoda in 1965. We taught together at a private school in Sands Point, New York, and he listened with interest when I talked about my childhood experiences in Cape Breton. When he learned about our travel plans in 1974, he asked to join us on our drive there. He was visiting some friends in Chebeague Island, Maine in Casco Bay, an open bay on the Gulf of Maine near Portland, Maine. We picked him up in Yarmouth, Maine and traveled along the mid-Maine coast visiting the historic villages along the way because Martin was knowledgeable about the historic homes in this picturesque region.

Martin was an entertaining storyteller, and Rhoda and I were often in stiches with his humorous observations as we drove toward Cape Breton. He stayed with us in Cape Breton for a few days and then flew out of Sydney airport to visit other friends in the Boston area the day President Nixon tearfully resigned (August 9th). Martin was spared the opportunity to take part in berry picking. After seeing Martin off, we had more time on our hands because we no longer had to show him some of the special places that we eagerly wanted him to see. Martin probably would not have wanted to do berry picking anyway.

Dad was quite ill at the time, and I made certain to bring several jars of raspberries and blueberries home to him. It made me feel good to see how he enjoyed eating Cape Breton raspberries and blueberries for the last time. It was very poignant for him as well as me. I hoped he regarded this small gesture as a thank you for giving me such marvelous summers in Margaree.

Rhoda and Mark Schwartz picking berries, August, 1974.

After our boys married and had families of their own, they joined us in Cape Breton in 2016 to help Rhoda and me celebrate our fiftieth wedding anniversary. We chose one day to pick blueberries near the Margaree Airport, a tiny plot of land with a single paved runway, near the village of Margaree Valley. The area had many low-bush blueberry plants, and the picking went well. All our grandchildren enthusiastically took part in the work. I thought back wistfully to many years before to the berry picking that my parents and their friends enjoyed so much.

Grandchildren Ari, Hannah, Sophie, and Vivi Schwartz
with their blueberries, August 2016.

Part of their haul, collected in August, 2016.

Chapter Six
Schoolhouses and General Stores in Margaree

W hat particularly interested me when I first visited Margaree in 1948 and in subsequent years was the numerous one-room schoolhouses and general stores that dotted the landscape of the Margaree Valley. At that time, almost every hamlet or village in the Margaree Valley had their own one-room schoolhouse and general store. I was accustomed to the large urban public school I attended in the heart of Queens, New York, which made this experience even more valuable for me.

One Room Schoolhouses

The cozy one-room schoolhouses in the Margaree Valley were something like pictures in the storybooks I read. Up to that point, I had never encountered these tidy structures. What made this even more exciting was the presence of a schoolhouse adjacent to Rose and her brother's farm. In front, it bore the sign, "Margaree Ford."

Nearly every village in the Margaree Valley had its own school. So, Margaree Forks, Margaree Harbour, and Northeast Margaree had their own one-room schoolhouse. These communities were incorporated villages, with a separate post office and stores. The schools were very similar to one another in size and shape. The buildings were usually faded white structures when I visited with my parents. They had rows of desks neatly arranged in aisles, with a teacher's desk in the front of the room. A blackboard and a map of Canada hung behind the teacher's desk and the Canadian flag hung in the front, "standing guard for thee." In the back there were hooks for children's coats as well as a wood-burning stove that kept the students warm during the cold winter months. I observed all this through the windows of the schools because they were locked during the summer months. I sometimes wondered how I would fare in a one-room school, thrown together with children of different ages, learning different skills.

As previously related, Margaree Ford was not actually an incorporated town or village but was the postal address given to Rose's farm because she served as a postmistress for the other farm families in the community. It was so named because it corresponded to the place in the Margaree River where farmers crossed or forded the river, thus the derivation of the name. A viable one-room schoolhouse gave this locale a vital presence in the Margaree Valley, even though there was no incorporated village.

Margaree Ford School, August 1966.

The schoolhouse in Margaree Ford, after it was closed and no longer served as a school in the late 1950s, was used as a storage facility by Rose's nephew, Alec Miller. Alec was a practical man who, after he inherited his aunt's farm, utilized such structures that no longer served as places of learning. So, the Margaree Ford schoolhouse was filled with the sort of family possessions people store in their attic. Miller subsequently rented it to summer guests to stay. One year, a visitor foolishly left the stove burning on a chilly day, and sadly the fire consumed the structure.

Chimney Corner, where we often went swimming, had its own school but no post office or any stores. In addition to its superb beach, there were a few farms nearby. The beach was wonderful, with nary a soul there. Dad often reminisced about Chimney Corner Beach when describing the delights of Cape Breton to colleagues, but he said nothing about the schoolhouse that was perched on a hill across the road that ran to the beach. During later visits, the school sat there forlornly, long after it was abandoned as a school, with its structure and sign intact.

Although the Chimney Corner school remained standing for a considerable time after it no longer served as a school, it was not utilized in any way. It was sad to witness its slow deterioration during our annual summer visits to the nearby beach. We wondered if the farmer who owned the property where the school was located would do anything to save it. He finally took it down one year, and all the desks, the blackboard, and the other furnishings were gone. The fate of the schoolhouses as well as the general stores encapsulate the changes that had occurred in the Margaree Valley, and indeed in many regions of rural Nova Scotia.

Sadly, these charming places of learning were abandoned

as a result of a series of school consolidations that took place in rural Nova Scotia beginning in the 1950s and 60s. One-room schoolhouses became relics of the past. After Nova Scotia abandoned the one-room schoolhouses all over the province, the provincial government continued their program of school consolidation in the rural regions of the province, including Cape Breton. Relatively small but traditional schools that had separate classrooms were closed in favor of larger regional schools because there were fewer children of school age in the rural areas, and now these schools served a larger geographical area.

In the 1980s, we noticed that there were handmade signs on barns and other buildings that had appeared, declaring "SOS," i.e. "Save Our Schools." This was the unhappy result of the demographic changes in Nova Scotia, especially Cape Breton. There were fewer farm families with fewer children. In spite of the school consolidations, Cape Bretoners continued to value their schools, maintaining a firm belief in the importance of their children's education.

By the time I returned to Cape Breton in 1963, these schools no longer served as places of learning for the children of the farm families in the region. Although considered obsolete, previously they had prepared students of past generations for higher education. Cape Breton and the rest of Nova Scotia was, and still is, notable for the large percentage of young people who go on to college.

Although the buildings no longer function as schools, some of the structures have remained intact for a considerable amount of time, sometimes serving as summer cottages or as storage places for farmers in the area. A few have been abandoned but there is one notable exception. The school building in Northeast Margaree was converted into a local museum in 1965, the "Margaree Salmon Museum." It eventually doubled in size when a new wing was added, and it remains a vital part of the community. It celebrates people like Marcel Tabuteau, and other musicians and artists as well as prominent physicians and writers, who came to Margaree to fish during their summer holidays.

Rhoda at the well outside the old Northeast Margaree School
during its expansion and conversion into the
Margaree Salmon Museum, August 1966.

Rhoda and I visited the museum often during our visits to Margaree. We became friendly with the museum curator, Frances Hart, who lived in the village of Margaree Centre. Every summer we stopped by and chatted with her, catching up with news concerning the Margaree Valley. During one of our visits, probably in the 1980s, the daughter of Frank DuMond paid a visit to the museum. She presented an oil painting by her father which depicted a fisherman angling in the Margaree. Frances set up a nook in the museum where she hung the painting, with articles about DuMond in art publications and hand-lists of exhibitions where DuMond's work was exhibited.

That inspired me to honor Tabuteau's memory. Although there was a black and white photo of him buried among other photographs of people who fished in the waters of the Margaree, there was no information about him and his importance in the music world. I contributed copies of several photographs that my father had taken in August 1948, including a color print of him holding a large salmon he had caught, standing near Rose's farmhouse. I included color prints of Susan and me with Tabuteau on his acres near Whale Cove. I also contributed a copy of his obituary from *The New York Times* from 1966, the year he passed away in France. I felt that someone of Tabuteau's stature should be recognized, and the copies of the photographs along with the other information about him are in a display case in the museum.

Interior of Margaree Salmon Museum
(Old Northeast Margaree School Building), 1990s.

Exterior of Margaree Salmon Museum, as it exists today.

The General Stores

Every one of the villages in the Margaree Valley had its own general store, and each store had a character all its own. They were not the glossy places that one still encounters in Vermont, for example, selling all the types of fudge and apparel you can find in L.L. Bean or the Vermont Country Store, marvelous places in their own right. The general stores in Cape Breton were more utilitarian, not geared to the tourist trade but places where the locals could find food and other staples.

Grocery stores and places called "candy stores" flourished in post-World War II New York. The so-called "candy stores" sold newspapers, magazines, toys, candy, soda, and baseball cards, and such stores seemed to be omnipresent in the Queens borough of New York City when I was young. My grandfather had a "candy store" in Richmond Hill, Queens, and my father and his two younger brothers worked many hours in the store while they were growing up. After the war, supermarkets began to flourish in Queensborough Hill (a neighborhood near the grounds of the World Fairs of 1939-40 and 1964-65) where I grew up, and they were markedly different from the all-purpose general stores that I discovered in Margaree.

Taylor's in Northeast Margaree had what is often referred to as "dry goods." Dad bought a pocketknife there that had been manufactured in Sheffield, England so he would be able to whittle or carve wood in the Acadian manner under Lou Cohen's expert direction. He seemed very pleased with his purchase, explaining to me that products made from Sheffield steel were of very high quality. In the late 1960s, a few years after Rhoda and I spent our honeymoon in Margaree, Taylor's store burned down, and he subsequently resurrected a smaller version of his store in an annex attached to his home in Northeast Margaree before he eventually retired. He had many interesting items in his original store besides pocketknives, or at least they seemed so to me as a young boy.

LeBlanc's in Margaree Forks had household items, smaller giftable items, and greeting cards. The store eventually sold larger items such as stoves and refrigerators. There, we bought postcards and the refreshing clear cream soda that was only available in Canada. When LeBlanc's store expanded its operation, selling modern appliances and other larger hardware items, its continued success seemed assured. However, about ten years ago, they went out of business.

The general stores were not designed for the tourist trade, but they filled an important need. MacPherson's in the hamlet of Margaree Valley, for example, sold fishing licenses, groceries, fresh produce such as meat and poultry, and postcards with photographs depicting the assorted landscapes of the Margaree Valley. Doyle's outside Margaree Forks had all sorts of fishing equipment and sold fishing licenses.

MacPherson's, in the town of Margaree Valley (originally named Frizzleton), remained in business until late in 2020, but the building still survives. I used to bicycle there from the nearby Normaway Inn where we stayed for many years. It was a white clapboard building where I bought the daily newspaper, the *Halifax Chronicle-Herald*, tea, as well as other items.

In addition to selling individual specialty items, all the stores sold the usual staple of groceries, newspapers, and "dry goods." The proprietors were friendly, and locals would go there to share local gossip and news. Doyle closed his store more than 40 years ago and the building was torn down, so people who wanted to fish in the Margaree generally bought their fishing permits at the Margaree Salmon Museum or MacPherson's. Traces of the stone foundation from Doyle's store still remain alongside the road outside of Margaree Forks.

Most of the stores have gone out of business with the exception of Laurence's in Margaree Harbour. Laurence's was owned by Hastings Laurence, a man with an almost aristocratic bearing. He was a dead ringer for actor John Houseman; he even sounded a bit like him. Laurence's store had smaller hardware items, school supplies, and food items such as cereal and sandwich meat. His son Fletcher still operates the store, and he also serves as postmaster for Margaree Harbour, a job given to him a dozen or so years ago, which he reluctantly accepted. Fletcher is a very genial man who has hung on, selling staples such as food, newspapers, and other essential items. He has an array of interesting postcards, including reproductions of old photographs of the area and paintings of local scenes done by Robert Selkowitz, an artist from Woodstock, New York who regularly spends his summers in Margaree.

In Margaree Centre, there was a general store I was not familiar with as a boy—Ingraham Brothers' Store. It had not served the community for quite some time and instead was a museum that never seemed to be open. One day when Rhoda and I were staying at the Normaway Inn, we took a ride to mail some postcards or perhaps buy some stamps. We noticed that the store/museum was open. This was not a serendipitous discovery on our part because there were circulars advertising its existence at the Inn.

On this particular day, not only was it open, but a friendly, elderly gentleman, C. Baxter Ingraham, seemed eager to have guests stop by. He explained that he was the last survivor in his immediate family, and that the store had not served as a general store for many years. He was operating it, in effect, as a museum, to illustrate to visitors what a general store was like in the Margaree area at the turn of the century (19th to 20th). His father and uncle founded the store in 1885, and he wanted their efforts in serving the community to be remembered. In its heyday, it offered all sorts of things that people in a farming community needed, most particularly hardware. Now, he had memorabilia for sale as well as records and documents depicting the local history of the area.

We enjoyed his stories about the community, and he explained that the store had operated until the depression when his father and uncle passed away. Ingraham took a liking to us and gave us a pad that was used by clerks to itemize and record the sales they made to customers. Rhoda and I found the situation touching and a bit sad while we listened to this kind old man. I thought that perhaps the way most of the general stores in the area closed was a better way of going out of business. In the next few years when we stayed in the area, I noticed that store/museum was never open. I was a bit apprehensive asking about C. Baxter Ingraham, and we assumed he passed away.

Ingraham Brothers Store/Museum, August 2006.

In later years, when we stayed in Margaree Centre—we rented a cottage at River Trail Cottages during the summers of 2013 to 2019—we became more familiar with a convenience store next to a service station that sold gasoline and repaired automobiles, "Ingrahams' Garage." We assumed it might be owned by relatives of C. Baxter Ingraham because there are many Harts and Ingrahams in the Margaree Centre area who are related to one another in some way.

The convenience store next to the service station is a newer store and is in a plain but more modern-looking building, which primarily sells food items such as oatcakes and scones that are made by local people. It also had a section that offered many different flavors of ice cream, including a variety of the maple-flavored ice cream, maple walnut, which we loved although it was not the plain maple-flavored variety that Rhoda and I had discovered—and happily devoured—on our honeymoon.

When Rhoda and I briefly visited Margaree in 2019, the building that had been occupied by LeBlanc's general store was still intact, but it remained abandoned, unable to compete with the development of larger cooperative stores (commonly referred to as COOPs) in the area. When I returned for an even briefer visit with Mark and George in 2022, the building was still standing, but it remained unoccupied.

MacPherson's General Store in Margaree Valley, August 2022.

The cooperatives which developed in the rural parts of Nova Scotia in the 1950s and later, made the general stores' position in the Margaree Valley untenable. These changes were part of a process that accelerated with the completion of the Causeway, connecting Cape Breton to the mainland of Nova Scotia. These COOPs have evolved into attractive supermarkets and in effect, sometimes serve as small department stores as well as hardware stores, often offering the items that were in one or another of the individual stores that so fascinated me when I was young, and into my adulthood. But as life became more complex, the needs of Cape Bretoners did as well. The Cooperatives do not have the warmth or charm of the general stores, which were commonly white clapboard buildings with shelves full of groceries and other items that the local people required. And the owners of the general stores were a friendly sort, who allowed visitors and the local folk continuity with the past.

Laurence's General Store, Margaree Harbour, August 2022.

[**Note**: Recently, *The New York Times* published a story (on November 29, 2024) about a country store in a rural region of Vermont, more than 25 miles from a larger grocery store. From the description in the story, it seemed reminiscent of the type of general stores that were common in the Margaree Valley. The story indicated that the proprietor and his wife wished to sell the store because they were too old to work the store any longer, but with the stipulation that the buyer must maintain the store so it would continue to serve the community as it had done before. This article reminded me of the general stores in the Margaree Valley and how they filled a vital function.]

Chapter Seven
The Normaway Inn

During our many visits to Cape Breton, Rhoda and I stayed at The Normaway Inn. Located in a beautiful valley surrounded by verdant hills, it is a few miles from Northeast Margaree. The postal address of the inn is Margaree Valley. When I visited Margaree with my parents and stayed at Rose Tompkins's farm, there was little reason to travel to the Normaway despite the attractiveness of the surrounding area. I vaguely recall that my parents and I ate there on one occasion.

Because Rhoda and I stayed at the Tompkins farm on our honeymoon in 1966, we had little need or desire to explore other lodging possibilities. We were mainly interested in searching for new and different places to eat. We once ate at the inn on our honeymoon but did not give any thought to staying there. When Rhoda and I went there for dinner then, in 1966, we observed its pleasant dining room, with windows that looked out on panoramic views of the valley. The food was good, though not particularly fancy, reflecting its rustic Scottish cuisine.

Afterward, we did not return to Cape Breton for eight years. Because Rose's heir to her farm, Alec Miller, required more space for his family, he no longer rented rooms in the farmhouse. When we planned our return to Margaree in 1974, we realized we had to make other arrangements.

Rhoda and I wanted comfortable accommodations and a place that would be close to the scenic vistas of the Margaree Valley. Our son Mark was now a year-and-a-half-old, and our good friend Martin Hutner accompanied us as well. He had heard me describe my summers spent in the Canadian Maritimes and was curious to observe Cape Breton's allure for himself, so he accompanied us. That is when we first stayed at the Normaway Inn, in 1994.

George MacPherson, who was born on the property, began operating the Normaway as an inn in 1928. Several of the Inn's buildings were constructed in the 1920s, and the property had for a brief period served as a religious retreat. A family from Sydney, the MacDonalds, purchased the property in the 1940s.

When we began staying at The Normaway Inn, I recalled Dad mentioning to me that on one occasion, all of us, including the Cohens, went to The Normaway Inn for dinner. All I remembered about the inn from my Cape Breton vacations with my parents was the horseshoe pit located in front of the main lodge.

Living Room at The Normaway Inn, late 1990s.

Although the inn was about ten miles from our favored swimming areas on the Gulf, it seemed well-suited to our needs. We took rooms in the main lodge adjacent to a commodious living room. The living room had some comfortable chairs, a large sofa, a stone fireplace, piano, and bookshelves stocked with a wide array of books and magazines. The property also had a number of attractive cabins.

David MacDonald, the son of one of the MacDonald brothers who owned the Inn, was a university student at the time and was helping run the place during the summer of 1974. He was very accommodating, and we found him interesting to talk to. While we were there that summer, there was much to talk about. The "smoking gun" tape revealing Richard Nixon's criminal conduct became news. Dave set up a television near the reception desk and guests watched Nixon's resignation speech. Years later, Dave recalled that scene to first-time visitors, indicating to guests how Rhoda and I shared that moment of history with him and other guests who were staying there in August 1974.

We returned to Cape Breton four years later, in 1978. We were touring New Brunswick and Prince Edward Island, and we wanted to go to Nova Scotia and briefly visit Cape Breton Island. In addition to Mark, we had our younger son, George, in tow. George was born just a year and a half earlier, and we named him after my father. Now as a family of four, we set out for the Maritimes. We stayed in one of the Normaway's cabins for our brief visit.

By then, Dave MacDonald had graduated from college, and his father and uncle had officially put Dave fully in charge of running the Normaway. Frankly, they wanted to unload the place. But locals were fearful that the beautiful property would be subdivided and haphazardly developed, and Dave did not want the family to let go of the property. He had all sorts of plans on how to run the inn.

Dave's vision was to turn The Normaway Inn into more than a late spring and summer vacation spot. It would be a destination for viewing the autumn colors and eventually a center for cross-country skiers. His plans were consistent with his family's business interests in Sydney; they owned a winter sports shop. He also planned to build a number of more modern cabins, i.e., "chalets" with hot tubs and other modern innovations. When he told me about the "chalets," I was a bit fearful. I thought the chalets would detract from the charm of the place. I was wrong. When they were built, they were located on the outer reaches of the Inn's grounds, and eventually they blended in with its surroundings.

Dave also wanted to turn the living room into a place for entertainment as well as a comfortable space where guests could chat with one another. Initially, he showed short films produced by the National Film Board of Canada. One film, *Song of the Seasons,* described a sheep farm in Mabou and the shearing that took place in early spring. The highlight was Raylene Rankin singing wistful Scottish folk songs in Gaelic. Raylene was a member of a talented family who performed chiefly in Canada. We got to know Raylene quite well when she worked at the front desk at the Normaway Inn during the summer of 1986.

The most memorable film for me was *Margaree People.* It was produced by an American photographer George Thomas—who taught a photography course at MIT—and it depicted the lives of local people, including Hastings Laurence, proprietor of the general store in Margaree Harbour. Another film, *Fixed in Time,* told the story of the 1917 explosion in Halifax harbor and the great fire that resulted through the eyes of a Halifax photographer of the period. The films provided guests with a good opportunity to learn about the history and culture of Cape Breton and Nova Scotia.

Dave began to invite local musicians to perform in the living room including fiddlers, step dancers, and folk singers. At the time, Cape Breton was experiencing the beginning of a musical renaissance. The post-war generation rediscovered the Gaelic tunes that their grandparents had embraced. Mom and Dad did not get to witness this aspect of Cape Breton culture. It was not until the late 1970s that this burst of musical creativity (and rediscovery) spread from the Maritimes to the United States. National Public Radio began broadcasting programs featuring Scottish and Irish folk tunes and devoted some of their playlists to Cape Breton music, an amalgam of Scottish, Irish, and Acadian music.

Folksinger Louis Arsenault performing in the
Normaway Living Room.

After his family gave Dave complete control over the Normaway in 1990, he inaugurated weekly barn concerts and square dancing during the height of the summer tourist season. The concerts attracted many local people as well. At the same time, many such events in the Margaree Valley began to fill churches and other venues. Dave refurbished an old barn on his property, and the weekly barn concerts and dancing attracted many people. Numerous musicians performed, and there were step-dancers and vocalists who sang many Scottish and Irish folk melodies.

The barn concerts became very popular, and people looked forward to the event. We frequently saw and heard the renowned fiddler Buddy Macmaster, who was already a local legend. He kept Cape Breton music alive during its lean years and inspired many musicians including his niece, Natalie Macmaster. Natalie, who was also an excellent fiddler, frequently toured the United States. We attended one such event on the New York City college campus where I taught.

Buddy Macmaster performing at a
Normaway Barn Concert in the late 1990s.

Buddy Macmaster performing at a
Normaway Barn Concert in 1996.

Dave also altered the dining room menu. He hired chefs whose specialty was gourmet cooking. The rich fair became too much for our tastes; we did not need the lavish four-course dinners the inn offered. For a number of years, we ventured out to various restaurants in Baddeck, Cheticamp and beyond, repeating what Rhoda and I did during our honeymoon. When Dave asked us why we no longer ate at the Normaway, we explained that with two young boys we preferred "home-style" cooking, with fresh salmon and other local fish. Dave often asked me advice about such matters as if my background as a New Yorker qualified me to offer such guidance.

Dave switched to a modified "American plan." Even before he changed his menu, we continued to enjoy the hearty breakfasts the inn offered, featuring its unique porridge bread and oatcakes, along with other delights such as fresh rhubarb that was grown on the Inn's grounds. Now, under a modified

"American plan," we began to eat dinner at the Normaway again. We found that we had more flexibility in planning the evenings we spent there. On special occasions, such as our anniversary or when family or friends joined us for their holiday, it proved to be a pleasant venue for such gatherings.

Cathy, Mark, Rhoda, Joel, George, and Janna
celebrating our 40th Anniversary, August 2006.

Dave began to diversify and acquire other properties. Eventually, his interest in The Normaway Inn began to wane. But we continued to stay at the Normaway because we were comfortable there. Often in the living room after dinner, we met many interesting people who were also staying at the inn, such as George Berry, the principal bassoonist with the St. Louis Symphony Orchestra. He retired from the orchestra in 2010 after serving in that capacity for 47 years. He and his wife, Marilyn, bought a summer home in the town of Mabou, Cape Breton. Now retired, he planned to use the opportunity of having more time to learn and master playing the Scottish bagpipes.

Before his retirement, while George Berry was an active member of the St. Louis Symphony, Rhoda and I attended a concert given by the St. Louis Symphony Orchestra at Carnegie Hall in New York. We enjoyed his virtuosity as he expertly played the bassoon. After the concert, we had a post-concert dessert with George and Marilyn at a charming cafe across the street from Carnegie Hall. We last saw George and Marilyn Berry in their new home in Mabou. That evening, we had dinner with them at the Rankins's restaurant in Mabou, the Red Shoe, and were treated to an evening of fiddling and Gaelic songs at the restaurant.

Rhoda standing in front of the Red Shoe Pub
in Mabou, August 2015.

There are still many fiddlers and folk singers to entertain guests and chances to meet people from many different parts of the United States and Canada at the Normaway Inn. And the extensive travel guide, *Doers and Dreamers*, which is revised annually and given free of charge at the Nova Scotia Tourist Center in Amherst, Nova Scotia, continues to rate the Normaway very highly. We stayed at the Normaway until 2013. When Rhoda's health began to decline, she wanted more privacy. We rented a cabin in the vicinity of Margaree Centre when we vacationed in Margaree in the summers after 2013.

The Normaway's influence was felt locally, and it continues to enjoy its status as a destination for tourists. Its barn concerts and dances remain popular with tourists and locals. In addition, several of the people who previously worked at the inn founded a breakfast and lunch place in Northeast Margaree, The Dancing Goat. It serves the wonderful breakfasts we previously enjoyed at the Normaway and offers excellent sandwiches made with the porridge bread we enjoyed at the Inn.

Rhoda, Mark, and George on the grounds of the Normaway,
August 1978.

Rhoda at The Normaway Inn, Summer 1986.

My Bicycle Trip Through the Margaree Valley

The author on a bike near back entrance of the
Normaway, early 2000s.

After he assumed full responsibilities of running the Normaway, Dave decided to buy bicycles in order to add activities at the Inn. I made ready use of one, a simple mountain bike that I rode to places in the nearby area. I frequently rode the bike to MacPherson's General Store in the evening after dinner to buy lollipops and mints for Rhoda and our boys. I found the ride exhilarating, with the cool evening air rushing in my face. It was a good prelude to the musical entertainment awaiting us that evening in the Normaway's living room.

Visiting my friend after my bike ride in Margaree, August 1992.

In August 1992, I decided to bike to all the towns in the Margaree Valley. It was a beautiful sunny day, and we had nothing planned. Thus, on that Sunday morning after breakfast, I set out on one of Dave's mountain bikes from the inn toward Northeast Margaree. I stopped briefly to say hello to Frances Hart at the Salmon Museum and pushed on to

Margaree Forks. Before reaching the Forks, I crossed the Margaree River on the twin bridges near where Doyle's General Store had stood many years before. I then entered the majestic panorama where the Margaree Valley seems to open up dramatically as I headed toward the Tompkins-Miller farm in Margaree Ford (Fordview). On the way, the retired thoroughbred horse who always seemed to look out of its barn window when we rode by in our car, greeted me.

I rode past Rose and Mike Tompkins' farm where I first stayed with my parents many years before, feeling more exhilaration, abetted by the strong breeze created as I picked up speed going downhill to Margaree Ford. Then I continued on to the village of Margaree (East Margaree). The terrain was relatively flat along the road on the eastern banks of the Margaree River. Then, after a mile or so, it became steeper and the going was tougher. I finally reached the bridge connecting the route I had been on with Margaree Harbour on the western bank of the Margaree River.

I crossed the bridge and rode into the village of Margaree Harbour. I chatted with Fletcher Laurence at his general store. I bought and drank a soda there to slake my thirst before leaving Margaree Harbour. I then doubled back to the main road, which is a part of the Cabot Trail.

I passed the rebuilt and modernized Duck Cove Inn and passed the Marple family farm, which we often visited. I met the Marples years before when I first visited Margaree with my parents. I spotted Winston Marple, someone I had known for many years, working on his tractor on the side of the road. I told him what I was doing, and he wished me luck and asked if I needed any assistance. I said I was fine, and although I was quite exhausted by this time and soaked with perspiration, I biked onward.

I gained energy as I biked past so many of the places I viewed from the car over the years. Now, I was able to take in the dramatic vistas of the Margaree Valley from the perspective of something akin to traversing the terrain on horseback. I rode into Margaree Forks and stopped by LeBlanc's General Store where I bought a bottle of that Canadian clear cream soda. Refreshed, I continued on to Northeast Margaree, stopping by the Salmon Museum to tell Frances Hart of my progress before I headed to the Normaway.

I reached the inn in midafternoon after my journey of approximately five hours on the bike. Rhoda and George greeted me. (Mark was in southeastern Turkey on an archeological dig.) We got in the car and I retraced my route, clocking the miles I had traveled on the bike. I observed that I rode 28 miles on the 3-speed bike, not bad for a 51-year-old.

The author after his 28-mile bike ride in
Margaree Valley, August 1992.

Eeyore at the Normaway

In 1994 or '95, Dave bought a young donkey for his wife, Theresa. Theresa McDonald was quite taken with the animal whom she named Eeyore, after the donkey in the A. A. Milne stories. Dave thought he would have Eeyore pull a cart to give rides to the children staying at the Inn. He never followed through with that plan and Eeyore was kept in the pasture with several horses that Dave cared for. The horses largely ignored Eeyore, but I am told that the donkey's very presence seemed to protect animals such as sheep and cattle from such predators as Eastern Coyotes.

We were also taken by Eeyore, and over the years, he greeted us because we fed him hay and carrots we obtained from the kitchen at the Inn. In the succeeding years we stayed at the inn and afterwards when Rhoda was ill, we frequently paid Eeyore a visit. Rhoda loved the animal, and he allowed her to hug him.

Rhoda and George with Eeyore at Normaway, August 1999.

Rhoda and the author with Eeyore, August 1999.

Rhoda with her friend, August 2001.

Rhoda with Eeyore, August 2006.

After Rhoda passed away, Mark, George, and I briefly went to Cape Breton in 2022, and we went to the Normaway to see how Eeyore was doing. He seemed to be a bit older but came over to us. I think he sensed somehow that his friend was missing.

Postscript about Raylene Rankin

We first met Raylene Rankin in 1986 when she was working at the front desk at the Normaway. She was a university student and was already well-known as one of "The Rankins," a group of brothers and sisters who performed in Canada. She was fluent in Gaelic and she sang many songs in that language. The Rankins hailed from Mabou where Gaelic was spoken frequently. Street signs in Mabou were in that language in addition to English in a determined effort to keep the dialect alive. We became friendly with Raylene when she worked at the Normaway. Rhoda often befriended people who worked and performed at the Inn.

Raylene grew bored with her job. She did not get a chance to sing there and was frustrated with the inefficiency she observed. Because she felt her talents were not being fully utilized, she decided to leave—but quietly, to avoid any ruffled feelings. We learned several years afterward that she arranged to have a friend from Inverness pick her up at the Normaway when she was not on duty. Because the Normaway is located off Egypt Road in the Margaree Valley, when she successfully made her departure and was no longer near the Normaway, she proclaimed, "I am out of Egypt, and I am in the promised land."

We last saw Raylene in 2005 when The Rankins were performing at the Village Gate in Greenwich Village in New York City. After the performance, we met with her, and she greeted us warmly. She amusingly talked about the time she spent at the Normaway, which she referred to as the "Canadian Fawlty Towers." By then, Raylene had graduated from the Dalhousie University law school. She was practicing law full-time but participated in her family's concert tours when she had the time to do so. She was impressed when we told her that our son, Mark, had gotten his Ph.D. the previous year, and that both our boys, whom she remembered when they were young, were now married. We told her that George was pursuing graduate work and would receive his doctorate several years afterward.

Raylene was much beloved by all who knew her for her charm and sense of humor. After we saw her in New York, we learned some years later that she became ill and passed away in 2012 at 52, leaving her husband and her young son.

Raylene Rankin in the late 1980s.

Chapter Eight
The Schooner Village

Another memorable experience from our vacations in Cape Breton was visiting the Schooner Village in Margaree Harbour. The Village was actually a delightful collection of shops that included the remnants of an old schooner, the *Marion Elizabeth*. The *Marion Elizabeth* was permanently berthed next to a wooden building that actually consisted of different but connected shops and a tearoom. The Schooner Village's shops were located near the approach road to the village of Margaree Harbour. If you did not take the road into Margaree Harbour but stayed to the right, you would cross a bridge at approximately the spot where the Margaree River flows into the Gulf of St. Lawrence. The bridge connected the village of Margaree Harbour on the western side of the Margaree River to the village of Belle Côte, which was located to the east and on the road that went northward toward Cheticamp.

When I first traveled to Margaree with my parents in 1948 and 1950, a small service station was all that existed on the site. When I returned with my future brother-in-law, Robert, in 1963, the service station was gone and in its place was a small restaurant that served breakfast and sandwiches. Ken Hannsford, a businessman from Toronto, had purchased the property and started a tourist shop in a log building he built in this well-situated location. The restaurant and shops grew from modest beginnings. The property included a small gallery, restaurant, and garden, and it became an attraction for tourists.

It was an advantageous location for visitors who were journeying toward Cheticamp and the Cape Breton Highlands National Park, where they could take in the majestic views of the Gulf of St. Lawrence and the Atlantic Ocean.

Hannsford commissioned various local artworks for his gallery. He took an interest in the work of Elizabeth LeFort, a prominent Cheticamp rug hooker. Eventually, Hannsford and LeFort married, and she demonstrated her craft in the small gallery on the property. Photographs taken by local photographers were displayed in the shop and gallery. The shop sold many vintage black and white photographs of the beautiful Margaree area, and the wonderful pictures he sold had the attribution, "Paul Pix." Eventually, the name Paul Pix was used when referring to the shop, gallery, and a store, which also sold newspapers and magazines. To complete this colorful scene, sometimes there was a young student playing the bagpipes in front of the bridge that crossed the Margaree River. Tour buses found this an excellent place to stop in the 1960s.

Paul Pix in the 1960s.

When Rhoda and I went to Cape Breton three years later for our honeymoon (1966), we found that the place had not changed much from three years before. I frequently stopped there to buy newspapers and magazines. I was able to keep up with events in the world beyond Margaree, for example, reading with delight about the triumph of the English soccer team that won the World Cup the previous week, in addition to other events occurring in the world in August 1966.

Eight years later in 1974, Hannsford sold the property to an American couple from Connecticut, John and Stephanie May. John May was a former executive with the Aetna insurance company. John and Stephanie were activists in the civil rights and peace movements in the United States in the 1950s and 1960s as well as in Great Britain where John May was born. When they took part in peace marches in Great Britain in the 1950s, they met the British philosopher Bertrand Russell, whom they corresponded with in subsequent years.

Disillusioned with the 1972 re-election of Richard Nixon and the continuation of the Vietnam War, the Mays decided to pull up stakes and move to Canada with their two children, Geoff and Elizabeth. They became enchanted with Cape Breton, having previously spent vacations there. Under their direction, the Paul Pix property in Margaree Harbour was modified. The building was expanded, and its exterior painted white, enhanced by a Tudor Revival style. The salvaged schooner ship, the *Marion Elizabeth*, was refurbished, and the restaurant also expanded while remaining attached to the main building.

The main building was subdivided into a number of small shops, each one selling specific goods: Scottish woolens, toys, women's clothing, and the like. Mark and George enjoyed looking at the toys and Rhoda enjoyed looking at the woolen goods. Over the years, I purchased Hudson Bay shirts in the woolen shop, and British metal soldiers (Marlborough Military Models) in the toy shop in addition to buying toys for Mark and George. When they were young, the May's children, Geoff and Elizabeth, helped serve homemade scones and other food. The Schooner Village also sold tapes of a large variety of Scottish music and other Gaelic tunes, often performed by local and other prominent artists.

John, Stephanie, and Geoff May in their shop in the Schooner Village, 1990s.

We became friendly with one of the women who worked in the shops, Eleanor Gillis. Ellie originally was from Ontario, and she and her husband had built a home in Scotch Hill, an area several miles north of Margaree Harbour. Ellie's home today remains a very warm and attractive place, located on a hill in its rustic setting. After Ellie's husband died, she has kept in touch with her children and friends via the internet when they are not able to visit.

Ellie was very much involved in Canadian politics, particularly in environmental issues. She sometimes supported the efforts of the New Democratic Party, the third party in Canada, whose strength historically has been concentrated in the Canadian prairies out west. We visited Ellie in her home during our visits to Margaree, and we discussed news about Margaree in addition to world-wide events.

Ellie Gillis with Rhoda, on the back porch of Ellie's home in Scotch Hill, August 2012.

An interesting attraction in the Schooner Village was the diorama that John May had set up with his personal toy soldier collection, depicting the battle of Waterloo. May was well-versed in the details of the pivotal 1815 battle in which the British and Prussian forces, as well as non-Prussian forces, defeated the French army, leading to Napoleon's second and final abdication. He hand-painted many of the soldiers in the display. The elaborate diorama was located near the front entrance.

In later years, Geoff developed programs where fiddlers and bagpipers would perform on the Schooner Village premises. Fiddler Buddy Macmaster, a leader in the music renaissance in Nova Scotia, gave one such performance which we were fortunate to attend. Geoff continued his family's interest in promoting Scottish culture, and they continued to sell some of the Paul Pix photographs.

Elizabeth May took a somewhat different path. Because of her family's commitment to environmental causes, she devoted her time and energy to these issues. She obtained her law degree from Dalhousie University. Influenced by her mother's political activities, Elizabeth became the founder and executive director of the Sierra Club of Canada. After resigning from that position, she stood for a seat in the Canadian parliament. She won a seat in the Canadian Parliament in a "riding," the Canadian term for a legislative district, west in British Columbia. She eventually became leader of the Canadian Green party.

After John and Stephanie passed away, Geoff May and his wife, Rebecca-Lynne, consolidated the shops and continued to live in their home in Margaree Harbour. Around 2002, the Nova Scotia highway department unveiled plans to build a new bridge replacing the old one, that would connect the western shore road with the eastern road. They determined that the best place for such construction would involve the property on which the Schooner Village was located. Geoff took a settlement from the provincial government and decided not to reestablish his business elsewhere in a different location. But he and Rebecca-Lynne remain active in promoting Gaelic culture and local crafts, as well as in their efforts for the protection of the environment.

We last saw Elizabeth about six years ago when she and her husband were celebrating their marriage together with Geoff, Rebecca-Lynne, and extended family at a restaurant in Belle Côte, the "Island Sunset." Rhoda and I spotted them at their family gathering in the restaurant, and we went over to their table to congratulate Elizabeth on both her marriage and her political career.

We have seen Geoff during our visits to Margaree and have enjoyed swapping insights about the condition of the world. He has retained his excellent sense of humor and remains an engaging person to talk with. Most of all, we very much regret the loss of the Schooner Village and the people whom we met there.

John May and a bagpiper, possibly Geoff, with the Schooner Village in background, 1990.

John May in front of his Schooner Village in 1990s.

Piper in front of Schooner Village, August 1999.

Chapter Nine
Cape Breton Highlands National Park: From the Gulf to the Atlantic and the Many Sites Along the Way

O ne of the delights for my family has been exploring other regions of Cape Breton. Although we were quite happy to spend time in the rustic setting of the Margaree Valley, we also took advantage of the good Cape Breton roads to visit the Fortress of Louisbourg, the city of Sydney, and especially Cape Breton Highlands National Park.

When I traveled to Cape Breton with my parents in 1948 and 1950, we did not leave the Margaree Valley very much. On occasion, with my father driving, we would go to the towns of Cheticamp and Baddeck. We only went to the Cape Breton Highlands National Park once in 1950. The park contains one of the most scenic drives in North America. The picturesque ribbon of road, winding around the mountain near the Park's western entrance, north of Cheticamp, has been captured in numerous photographs. When my father undertook the trip, probably in August of 1950, driving on this road was quite foreboding. It consisted of a narrow dirt road.

The Park was established in 1936. The road around the Park is often referred to as the "Cabot Trail," though in reality, a good deal of the Trail lies outside the Park, from south of Margaree in the western part of the Island—along the shores of the Gulf of St. Lawrence, to the area south of Ingonish Beach on the Atlantic Ocean. Lining the craggy coastline, the scenic highway in the Park offers sweeping ocean views, with hills, river canyons, valleys, and forests. There is an abundant amount of wildlife to observe, including many bird species and other animals such as moose and black bears. In the Park's southeast corner lies sandy Ingonish Beach, with the popular Keltic Lodge, which still today draws many visitors.

Dad followed the suggestion of many—local folks as well as park rangers—and drove in a clockwise direction, from the Park's western entrance several miles north of Cheticamp to the eastern entrance south of the town of Ingonish. After leaving the Park, there are still many miles to travel, although the driving is less taxing because the terrain is flat. The area outside the Park is sparsely populated.

When I traveled with Mom and Dad to the park in 1950, we gazed out at dense forests through the car's windows. We made our way westward toward Baddeck. None of us spotted any black bears, but my father, as an accomplished naturalist, identified a number of bird species, including kingfishers and eagles.

The dirt road in 1950 made the drive difficult. Also, because the road was so narrow, if an automobile was coming in the opposite direction, one driver would have to either back up or go forward to find a pull-off. However, the traffic was light in those days, minimizing the problem of such maneuvering. In addition, other drivers were very courteous. Nevertheless, Dad was glad to have traveled this challenging territory once. Our drive through the park in 1950 was our only visit there as a family.

In subsequent years, I have driven the same route almost every summer we have visited Cape Breton. The road is now well-paved and has two lanes. There is also more traffic. Some visitors do not follow the suggestion in guidebooks and by word-of-mouth, and take the journey in a counterclockwise direction, so the two lanes are a necessity. There are also abundant stops along the way where people can park their cars and hike to picturesque vantage points. Sometimes native animals can be observed.

During these later years, we have become more cautious because hybrid creatures—part wolf and part coyote, sometimes referred to as Eastern Coyotes—have been sighted, and there have been some incidents in which visitors have been attacked in the more remote parts of the Park. The Eastern Coyotes are more aggressive than the coyotes from western North America. The hybrid creatures developed when western coyotes migrated eastward and mated with the wolf populations in the rural northern parts of the eastern United States as well as eastern Canada. Fortunately, we had no such encounters with these wolf/coyotes.

Cap Rouge, Cape Breton Highlands Natural Park,
looking southward, August 1963

When I visited Cape Breton with my future brother-in-law, Dr. Robert Davidson, during the summer of 1963, I drove through Cape Breton National Park for the first time. Robert was still a medical student at the time and was captivated by the majesty of the landscape viewed from the highway. We both took numerous pictures, and later, Robert framed one of the brilliantly colored ones he photographed. It still adorns his medical office. The photograph of the twisting mountainous road along the shores of the Gulf was a graphic reminder of his experience.

Robert did not need even the gentlest persuasion from Susan to return to Cape Breton, as he had been quite captivated by the scenery in the park. In 1964, when they made their honeymoon in Cape Breton, they spent time there. In 1966, Rhoda and I also honeymooned in Cape Breton, and on a number of occasions, we went to Cape Breton Highlands Park because it was an exciting adventure for Rhoda, who was very much an urban dweller.

The drive through the national park is a day-long excursion, because even after leaving the park, there is considerable driving ahead if you are returning to the Margaree Valley or beyond. During the many summers that we vacationed in Cape Breton, we drove through the park, and on some occasions hiked at recommended locations, while enjoying the scenic vistas.

On the drive through the park, the last glimpse of the Gulf of St. Lawrence is in the town of Pleasant Bay. Although there is a road going further north, that portion is more remote and not well traveled. After going through Pleasant Bay, the recommended route is to travel in an eastward direction toward Cape North where we observed our first glimpse of the Atlantic Ocean. Then we drove southward toward the town of

Neil's Harbour and Ingonish along the Atlantic coast. In a matter of minutes, we were able to go from the gulf to the Atlantic, traveling the width of Cape Breton. The Atlantic seems to have a more aqua hue than the gulf, but the contrast is not so striking compared to the experience of being able to go from one large body of water to another in just a few minutes. Then, after going through Ingonish and its wonderful beach—and stopping at the famous and spectacularly situated Keltic Lodge—we went inland again in a westward direction toward St. Ann's and Baddeck.

Neil's Harbour inspired Sam Moon, a rock singer who grew up in the area, to write a folk tune while he was performing in Alaska and was homesick for Cape Breton. He wanted it to be something that would appeal to the musical tastes of his father's generation. The work, "Girls of Neil's Harbour," has been recorded, and it has become a popular tune.

Cap Rouge looking northward, Cape Breton Highlands National Park, August 1963.

Our traveling in the park has always been an enriching experience. The scenic vistas, the recommended hikes, and other attractions outside the park, have reinforced our appreciation of Cape Breton. At the western entrance of the park, a few miles north of Cheticamp in the visitors' center, there is a good description of the wildlife one might encounter in the park, complete with dioramas graphically illustrating the fauna and flora native to the area. There is also a good bookstore, offering books about the park, the wildlife, and the history of the region. The small towns located along the way that lie outside the park allow the trip to be broken up, helping visitors to not be too fatigued by their drive.

The Gaelic Mòd

Mounties at Gaelic Mòd, August 1950.

The Gaelic College in St. Ann's lies approximately eleven miles east of Baddeck. During the summer months, the college offers a two-week immersion course in many different aspects of Highland Gaelic culture, which is taken by young people of Scottish background. They learn Scottish dancing, bagpiping, and fiddling. At the end of their immersion in Scottish Highland culture, they perform at the Gaelic Mòd, an event held annually during the first week of August. Guest performers from Scotland entertain the audience. I first attended the Mòd with my parents in 1950, although I confess I was most transfixed by the sight of the Royal Canadian Mounted Police in their bright red regalia. I took several pictures of them, and frankly, that was my most enduring memory of attending the Mòd. Rhoda and I went to the Mòd on our honeymoon, and we took Mark and George there several times as well.

Piper at the Mòd, August 1950.

Young Dancers at Gaelic Mòd, August 1966.

Cheticamp

We often visited Cheticamp, not only on our excursions to the Cape Breton Highlands National Park, but to look at the different shops, particularly those that offered hooked rugs and other local crafts. Cheticamp was a fishing village with numerous small sailing crafts tied up at their docks. Over the years, commercial fishing out of Cheticamp declined, and fewer boats could be observed there. But a variety of stores have survived, including the COOP there, which has grown considerably in size and has a variety of groceries as well.

The COOP in Cheticamp is the busiest and best stocked store in the area. We often stopped by to buy certain everyday items, such as the unusual wintergreen toothpaste that is only sold in Canada. We also dropped by to see Louis Arsenault, the folksinger who performed at the Normaway on his guitar, whom we became friendly with. Louis's regular, full-time job was supervisor in the hardware department at the COOP.

We went to Cheticamp on numerous occasions to eat in several of the restaurants in the area. The seafood was fresh and reflected the French art of cooking and preparing meals. There were a variety of restaurants in the area, offering mainly seafood and freshwater fish. The restaurants were not fancy and were reasonably priced, and several catered to families with children, so our grandchildren enjoyed eating there. There are also several *boulangerie* in Cheticamp, so we have sometimes indulged ourselves in sampling the French bread and fresh brioches offered in these places.

Fishing Boats in the Village of Cheticamp, August 1963.

On the way to Cheticamp, we stopped at Flora's. On our honeymoon in 1966, we bought a hooked rug from her before she had her own shop. At the time, local craftswomen sold their products out of their own homes. In subsequent years, Flora opened her own shop, and as her business grew, she sold not only the rugs she made, but also the rugs hooked by other local artisans. When she started her store, Flora or her daughter were positioned near the entrance, demonstrating their craft at the loom. Flora's daughter has maintained that tradition, so there is generally somebody hooking rugs at their loom at the entrance. Now, Flora's has all sorts of goods for sale, including many souvenirs such as postcards, calendars, and clothing produced in the Province of Nova Scotia. Attached to the building, which has grown to two stories, there is a snack bar serving light meals and ice cream that my grandkids particularly enjoyed when they joined us for our 50th anniversary in 2016.

Baddeck

The village of Baddeck, with its distinctive Scottish flavor, is quite different from Cheticamp, which has a predominant Acadian population. There are restaurants, clothing shops, an antique shop, a museum, a fine local library, and the Alexander Graham Bell Museum. Bell spent many summers in Baddeck, and the museum displays many of the airplanes he designed in the early 1900s.

The pier on Lake Bras d'Or—actually a saltwater estuary—has grown from its plain wooden structure when I visited Baddeck with my parents. It is now a much more substantial concrete structure that houses several shops, sailing vessels such as sloops and schooners, and even a few large yachts.

One summer, we discovered the *Amoeba*, a 67-foot schooner, captained by John Bryson and built by his father more than 50 years ago. Bryson daily conducted several tours on the schooner. Several times, we went on Bryson's tour, highlighting Beinn Bhreagh, the Bell home, and wildlife, particularly eagles overhead. Bryson made these excursions entertaining with his engaging sense of humor, and we enjoyed the thrill of sailing on sparkling Lake Bras d'Or with many watercrafts on its glistening waters.

Sailing Regatta on Lake Bras d'Or, Baddeck, late 1980s.

Baddeck Pier, late 1980s.

Rhoda looking out at Lake Bras d'Or, August 1966.

John Bryson presenting instructions during sail, Summer 2006.

Rhoda, Mark, and George on Baddeck Pier with Lake Bras d'Or in background, Summer 1981.

Alexander Graham Bell Home, Beinn Bhreagh, Summer 1980s.

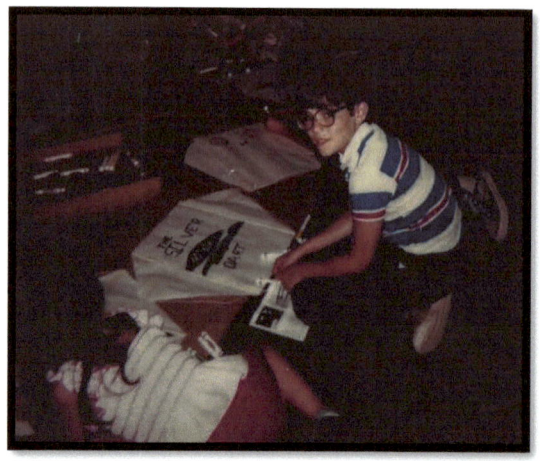

Mark at Bell Museum designing a new plane, August 1983.

All of us enjoyed visiting Baddeck. In the past forty years, upscale clothing stores have sprouted up, offering a variety of goods and sportswear. There are several nice seafood restaurants there as well that offer diners a beautiful view while eating. The Bell Museum, always worth a visit, has numerous child-friendly activities and features exhibits depicting the inventor's impact on the area. We took our grandchildren to the museum when we visited Cape Breton. In addition, the local library offers programs for children which our grandchildren enjoyed.

Mark and George particularly enjoyed going to Stone's drugstore, a rather large emporium selling a variety of things. I remember the store from my childhood. It was then a more traditional pharmacy which eventually grew in size. Until recently, it had a large array of toys and many American and Canadian magazines, as well as different souvenirs. My father bought me a miniature replica of a birch bark canoe there during one of the summers we visited Baddeck. It still remains in my possession and reminds me of our visits to Baddeck.

Stone's drugstore remains the same in size, but it offers larger items such as appliances, with fewer toys, souvenirs, and magazines, reflecting the changes that have taken place in recent years, such as the development, the growth, and the reach of the internet.

Fortress of Louisbourg

Rhoda and I first visited the Fortress of Louisbourg on our honeymoon in August 1966. When we visited the site then, roughly 25 miles from Sydney on the Atlantic Coast, it consisted of a museum building constructed in the 1930s and markers laying out the streets where reconstruction of the buildings of the fortress would take place. When we returned to Louisbourg with Mark and George in the 1980s, the reconstruction of this important piece of Canadian history had largely been completed.

We were able to tour at our own pace, and each site had knowledgeable guides who were very informative and gave very lucid explanations of the different places. There were no attempts to sell products, and the guides were very eager to answer questions posed by visitors—quite a contrast to some of the experiences we have had in other historic places. We enjoyed visiting this remnant of what once was a bastion of French Canada and had some empathy for the soldiers quartered in this cold, austere place that was so many miles from their home years before.

When the British conquered Louisbourg, they destroyed all the buildings in their effort to rid the area of all French influence. But some French settlers remained, and the reconstruction of the fortress that has taken place is a remarkable achievement. It has made the history of the region come alive.

Entrance to Fortress of Louisbourgh, 1990.

Main Street in the fortress, 1990s.

Mark and George on fishing vessel, summer 1986.

Street Performers, Louisbourg, Summer 1986.

Governor's Palace, Fortress of Louisbourg, late 1980s.

Drawing Room at Governor's Palace.

Chapter Ten
Reunions and Fishing in the Margaree

What perhaps is obvious in my narrative of summers in Margaree so far is that although I have frequently referred to others that have fished, I have not mentioned my family engaging in this activity. The reason is that no one in my immediate family was particularly interested in fishing, although Dad admired those who engaged in freshwater fishing (fly-fishing). When I accompanied Dad on field trips to the kettle ponds in Cunningham Park and Oakland Lake in Queens, New York, he carried a plankton net with him. When boys who were fishing in those places asked him what he was looking for, he replied, "I am interested in something smaller than fish."

Dad certainly was. He was interested in the microscopic world in a drop of water. He carried a magnifying glass with him and was able to get a rough view of the microscopic organisms he collected. When we got home, he would make slides of the pond water he collected and examine this microscopic world more acutely with his Zeiss microscope, his pride and joy. If there was something of special interest, he would photograph the unusual microorganisms he had collected.

But he never fished, nor did the rest of us. When we first traveled to Margaree in 1948 and 1950, we did not engage in fishing and neither did the Cohens. Lou Cohen did organize clam digging in Margaree Harbour Beach, but no one we knew joined people like Tabuteau in fishing for salmon or trout in the waters of the Margaree. During the many summers my family spent in Margaree, none of us expressed any interest in engaging in this activity. Mark may have mentioned trying his hand at it once or twice. He was perhaps the most adventurous of any of us, but we did not fish in Margaree's waters. We observed others who were busily engaged in fishing, but we never discussed any aspect of fly fishing with them except perhaps during our visits to the Salmon Museum in Northeast Margaree. That is, until 2004.

Robert and Susan joined Rhoda and me in June 2004 to celebrate their 40th wedding anniversary in Cape Breton. Robert's father was an avid fisherman, in salt water as well as fresh water. When Robert and I went to Cape Breton in 1963, fishing did not cross our minds. When Susan and Robert returned the next year on their honeymoon, to my knowledge, they did not fish.

Years ago, Robert took up the sport of fly-casting to relax from his arduous medical practice in Los Angeles. He took vacations in northern California and Montana where he applied his skills to the sport. Thus, in 2004, he was prepared to try his hand fishing in the Margaree River. And I would join him. We obtained fishing permits (short-termed licenses) from Frances Hart at the Salmon Museum in Northeast Margaree and employed a guide for the morning activity.

We went to a fishing pool just north of Margaree Forks, across the road from a farm I had driven by frequently. I would like to report that for the first time in my life, I caught a fish, but I had no such luck. The few times in my life that I have fished, I have not caught anything, except perhaps a cold. Not only that, Robert, who had developed considerable skill in the sport, came up empty-handed; he failed to catch anything. But it was an experience nevertheless, and I could finally say I went fishing in the waters of the Margaree.

The author with fishing regalia, June 2004.

Dr. Robert Davidson fishing in the Margaree River, June 2004.

Rhoda and I had a wonderful visit with Susan and Robert. We all stayed at the Normaway Inn, visited what remained of Rose's farm, drove to Cape Breton Highlands National Park, and hiked there as well. We celebrated their 40th anniversary with dinner at the Keltic Lodge in Ingonish.

The author with Susan (Schwartz) Davidson at Mike Tompkins barn, Margaree Ford, August 1948.

The author with Susan Davidson, in back of Mike Tompkins's barn, Margaree Ford, June 2004.

Susan and Robert at Cap Rouge, Cape Breton Highlands
National Park, June 2004.

The Fish Hatchery

The fish hatchery in Margaree is the oldest in Nova Scotia. It is located on the road to Big Intervale, which is accessible off the Cabot Trail near the borderline between the villages of Margaree Valley and Margaree Centre. The hatchery in Margaree has been important in keeping the Margaree waters well stocked with salmon and trout for years. The hatchery has worked with the Margaree Salmon Association to develop a Margaree River Collaborative Watershed Plan, designed to help maintain the fish population and the environment in the Margaree Valley. It is a rather modest-looking place that nevertheless plays a vital role in protecting the Valley's important resource.

I have few memories of the hatchery from when I visited the place with my parents and the Cohens in 1950, save for the few plain wooden buildings and the pools of water stocked with salmon and trout that constituted the facility. I do remember the sinister-looking metal cylinders on some of the trees on the property. Dad asked one of the people in charge at the hatchery a question concerning the purpose of these cylinders. The answer was that they were in place to reduce the population of kingfisher birds because those species of birds were deemed to be a threat to the salmon and trout in the hatchery. I vividly remember the gruesome explanation given on how these traps kill the birds—they break their necks! I never figured out how those metal cylinders operated but was much disturbed upon hearing this.

Dad diplomatically explained to the people at the hatchery that kingfishers did not pose a serious threat to the fish populations there, but inflicting unnecessary and cruel harm on the marvelous birds would upset the careful balance of nature that had been established. Apparently, this may have made an impression because when Rhoda and I visited the hatchery years afterward in 1966, I observed that there were no bird trap devices on the trees. I asked the people in charge what happened to the traps and was told that they learned years ago that they were not effective in protecting the fish but inflicted cruel punishment on the birds.

Chapter Eleven
The People of Margaree

Cape Breton is a land I know, where people with splendid hearts go.

My narrative about the people of Margaree is not limited to the many well-known artists, musicians, and other creative folk who summered on Cape Breton Island. It is also important to include the local people we became friendly with, people who made our holidays in Margaree so memorable and often made significant contributions in their chosen fields. My family befriended Cape Breton people whose roots run deep whether they were native Cape Bretoners or people like us, who discovered Cape Breton for themselves and returned frequently to this remarkable place. They were an integral part of our Cape Breton experience as well.

With the exception of Marcel Tabuteau (and Frank DuMond, whom we never met but whom was a mentor to my mother's friend, Hannah Cohen), we did not come into contact with many of the "famous" artists and other celebrities who bought property in the Margaree and Mabou area, making this area their second home. They were sometimes spotted buying groceries or shopping for necessities. Their privacy was generally respected.

The Well-Known Personalities of Cape Breton

The composer Philip Glass, artist Richard Serra, comedic actor Alan Arkin, documentary photographer Robert Frank, abstract artist June Leaf, slime mold expert John Tyler Bonner, and Michael A. Roosevelt, grandson of President Franklin D. Roosevelt, were just some of the well-known part-time Cape Bretoners. Michael Roosevelt was the son of James Roosevelt, who assisted FDR in simulating a walk when he took part in certain public events—FDR was often pictured during his presidential years leaning on his son.

F.A.O. (Fritz) Schwarz and his wife stayed at the Normaway Inn and later bought property in the Baddeck area. Dave MacDonald introduced Fritz Schwarz and his wife to us one summer, and when we spotted him at the barn concerts at the Normaway Inn, he gave us a warm hello. He was the chief council to Senator Frank Church (D-ID) when the Church committee investigated wrongdoing in the CIA and other security agencies in the 1970s, years before we were introduced to him at the Normaway.

Other notables include performance artist Joan Jonas, who was recently the subject of lengthy article in *The New York Sunday Times* (March 24, 2024). She bought a summer home on a hill overlooking the Gulf of St. Lawrence in the early 1970s. Although the article, "Island Home as Canvas and Stage" did not indicate its precise location, the pictures in the article suggest to me that her house is near Chimney Corner Beach. Jonas first arrived in Cape Breton in 1970 and has spent many summers there since then. A retrospective of her multimedia career includes images of her "Nova Scotia Beach Dance." When we drove down the road to go swimming, we were unaware of her performances there, or that there were select audiences attending her performances from the distance of a nearby cliff.

In the summer of 1950, Dad met Donald Goodchild, a scholar who was a member of the American Council of

Learned Societies. Goodchild and his wife Mayna lived most of the year in Vermont, and in Princeton, New Jersey, when he taught at Princeton University. On a trip to Cape Breton, they fell in love with Margaree and purchased property less than a mile from Margaree Harbour. They built a small but attractive gingerbread-style house on a hill overlooking the Margaree River. It required considerable work because the property had some boulders that had to be removed. Mayna Goodchild injured herself in the process of clearing their land, and Donald Goodchild wrote and privately published a short monograph chronicling Mayna's recovery.

Dad was fascinated by the small printing press that Goodchild owned. He employed it in publishing a weekly newspaper describing the people and local events in Margaree. Goodchild indicated that despite his poor health, he and Mayna would spend the winter in Margaree. I remember the following winter at breakfast while Dad was reading the newspaper (in early 1951), he learned the sad news that Goodchild had passed away. Mayna did not return to Margaree on a regular basis and eventually settled in Maryland. Their brightly-painted red home remains, well-tended by its current owners, who may be unaware of the entire story behind their strikingly elegant house.

Rhoda and I got to know George C. Thomas. Thomas had taught photography at MIT and eventually moved full-time to Margaree Harbour. He photographed many local people from the Margaree Valley: farmers, fiddlers, and artisans such as blacksmiths. He also photographed the owners of several general stores in the area, including Hastings Laurence, proprietor of the general store in Margaree Harbour. Thomas selected forty-eight black and white photographs—the heart of his collection of negatives and transparencies—for his book,

Margaree, and devoted a page to each subject. His intention was to photograph his neighbors and friends in order to preserve a record of a sadly vanishing world. The Canada Council for the Arts supported Thomas's work.

The National Film Board of Canada produced a film bringing the book to life. In the film, *Margaree People*, Thomas briefly interviewed the people depicted in his marvelous photographs. I bought the book in paperback form and asked Hastings Laurence to sign under his picture. Another picture in Thomas's book was of some members of the Tompkins family, including the children who had still lived on Rose's farm at the time. The children were perched on the same tractor where I sat during my first summer in Margaree in 1948 and on my honeymoon in 1966.

One summer, likely in the early 1980s, Thomas took some visitors, including me, out on his sloop to sail around Margaree Harbour. It was exciting because it gave us a different view of the houses and other property of Margaree Harbour, and Thomas made the sail quite special with his commentary.

We got to know Thomas through Myles Kehoe. Myles opened up an antique shop, "Myles from Nowhere," in Margaree Forks about thirty years ago. He was not native to the area but got to know many local people there. He was always friendly, and in recent years we stopped by his shop to learn the latest local news. About fifteen years ago, Myles had a reception where he invited many people to commemorate his years owning the shop. Unfortunately, that particular summer, we arrived in Margaree about a week too late, thereby missing the reception Myles held. According to Myles's description of the event, a number of people like Alan Arkin attended the party. Rhoda and I regretted not meeting some of these famous people.

When we visited the Margaree Salmon Museum in the early years, as related in a previous chapter, I discovered that there was only one photograph of Tabuteau and no mention of his importance in the musical world. The museum had the fly collections of some of the prominent people who fished in the Margaree, such as baseball Hall-of-Famer Ted Williams, but it did not contain samples of Tabuteau's collection. There were also photographs of fairly well-known people, such as prominent physicians who came to Margaree to fish, but there was next to nothing about Tabuteau.

I thought that Tabuteau deserved some recognition. Frances Hart encouraged me to contribute copies of pictures of Tabuteau, his obituary from *The New York Times*, and a short piece I wrote, explaining his significance as a world class musician which Frances Hart placed in one of the Museum's display cases.

Rhoda with Frances Hart at front desk at the Margaree Salmon Museum, early 2000s.

As I indicated, this idea was sparked by a chance meeting Rhoda and I had with Frank DuMond's daughter at the Museum. On that occasion, DuMond's daughter presented one of her father's paintings to the Museum. The painting depicted a local fishing scene in Margaree. In a corner of the Museum, Frances arranged a display under DuMond's painting, and she filled a table with magazine articles, catalogues, and hand lists of several shows he gave in New York in the 1940s and 50s. It vividly captures how DuMond spent his summers in the Margaree Valley where he found the peace and serenity that many have sought from this special place while he fished and painted. DuMond had also painted a portrait of Rose Tompkins that was purchased by an art dealer from Connecticut.

Kevin Tompkins with Susan in Rose's buggy in front of Rose's home, August 1950.

I learned about the existence of this work from Dr. Kevin Tompkins, who was Rose Tompkins's nephew. Kevin grew up on the Nova Scotia mainland and went to Dalhousie University medical school in Halifax, Nova Scotia. He became a professor of obstetrics and gynecology at McMaster University's medical school in Hamilton, Ontario. It was through Frances Hart that I began to correspond with Kevin. He had worked on his Aunt Rose's farm in 1950 when he was in his middle-teen years. I remembered Kevin from our stay on Rose's farm although I was only nine that summer. I also had taken a few pictures of him and sent him some of the black and white prints of him sitting in Rose's buggy with Susan in front of Rose's home. We started to write to one another, recalling our visits and his memories of spending summers working on the farm as well as our reflections on American, Canadian, and British politics.

Kevin also had vivid memories of Tabuteau's vacations in Margaree. He helped one of Tabuteau's students, Laila Storch, a distinguished oboist herself, with stories for a chapter about Tabuteau's holidays in Margaree for her biography of Tabuteau. Storch lived in the Seattle area. Thus, she did not get the opportunity of visiting Cape Breton and discovering a different aspect of Tabuteau's life and career. Kevin's memories supplied useful information about the summers Tabuteau spent on vacation in Margaree for her biography of Tabuteau.

Although we corresponded for over a decade, we never met until Kevin traveled to Margaree in 2000 or 2001 at the same time we were in Margaree on vacation. He joined us for breakfast at The Normaway Inn where we were staying that summer. We marveled that Kevin traveled all the way from Hamilton, Ontario on his motorcycle. We promised one another that we would meet again fairly soon.

Kevin invited us to visit and stay at his home in Hamilton but unfortunately that was not to be. Tragically, Kevin fell while hiking with a friend in the Niagara Gorge in Ontario, Canada in June 2003, and died from the injuries he suffered. He was 70. Frances Hart told us the sad news of his passing that summer when we visited Margaree. *The Toronto Globe and Mail's* obituary of Kevin detailed his distinguished medical career and ended by stating that he had always remained "loyal to his Cape Breton roots."

Friendships with the People of Margaree

We enjoyed the friendship of many in the area. The Cohens were friendly with the Marple family who had a farm between the village of Margaree (now called East Margaree) and Margaree Harbour, on the western bank of the Margaree River. Young Beatrice Cohen played with several of the Marple children. My sister went with Beatrice at the beginning of our stay in Margaree in 1948. Afterwards, I went with Mom and Dad to visit the Marple farm. Their house was located on a dirt road that wound up a hill overlooking the river valley. John Marple was a large and gentle man whom my parents liked immediately. His wife, Cristina, was outgoing, and over the years we stopped by to visit her.

I introduced Robert to the Marples when we visited in 1963. When I returned with Rhoda on my honeymoon in 1966, John Marple greeted us warmly and commented that I had gained some weight since he last saw me. I guess married life agreed with me. I last saw John Marple that summer when we drove away from their property after saying goodbye to the family. He was explaining something to his grandson at his barn alongside the road. John Marple passed away before we revisited Cape Breton in 1974. In subsequent years when we visited Margaree, I have thought about that poignant scene when I drive past the very spot where I last saw John Marple with his grandson.

But Mrs. Marple—as we always referred to her—remained alive for more than thirty years afterward, and we visited her every summer to catch up on local events. She often had one of her younger daughters or nieces staying with her. She served us tea and was as sharp as ever well into her nineties, beating the kids at Uno, a card game they all enjoyed playing. On the wall there were prints of pictures my father took many years before of members of her family. My mother had sent them to the Marples in the early 1950s, and they occupied an honored place, directly under a portrait of Great Britain's Queen Elizabeth.

Mom (Hannah Schwartz) with John and Cristina Maple,
August 1950.

125

The Marples' son Winston and I have remained in touch over the years. He and his wife Jeannine live on the property he inherited from his parents, but he no longer does any farming. During holiday season every year, we exchange greeting cards with a brief note expressing our wishes to one another for a good New Year.

Closer to The Normaway Inn, we became friendly with another farm family. Lorraine Fraser lived on her husband's family farm, Windy Valley Farm, right off Egypt Road just a mile from The Normaway Inn. Lorraine worked for Dave MacDonald at The Normaway Inn for a number of years, and she and Rhoda became friendly. Lorraine was insightful and an excellent conversationalist with a humorous outlook on life. In later years, we visited Lorraine's farm, and Rhoda enjoyed checking on the pigs, horses, and other farm animals that Lorraine and her husband Robbie kept. When Mark, George, and I returned to Cape Breton in 2022, the year after Rhoda passed away in 2021, Lorraine commented that she had realized that Rhoda was not herself a few years before when she had visited for the last time in 2019, because Rhoda had not asked Lorraine to see the pigs on her farm.

Lorraine and her husband supplied some of the food served at the Normaway. Their farmhouse had gained some notoriety years before, because it was originally located on a hill much higher than the valley where it is presently situated. Some ancestors of the Frasers moved the farmhouse down to where the barns were located. This herculean effort took place many years ago, before I ever visited Cape Breton. The move was a sensation at the time, and the feat made nation-wide Canadian newspapers. It is still regarded with some awe.

On Rhoda's last visit to Lorraine and her farm in 2019, she gave Rhoda a copy of Bob Woodward's book, *Fear:*

Trump in the White House. Lorraine found Trump so repellent that she wanted the book out of her house, even though it was quite a negative portrayal of him. We reluctantly accepted the book, indicating that we were only too aware of Trump's failings and how much damage he had done. When we left Nova Scotia a week later, we spotted a copy of a book by Julia Child at a fair in Maine, which I sent to Lorraine to reciprocate her generosity, explaining that it would be more uplifting.

Rhoda with Lorraine Fraser on her farm. Windy Valley Farm, Margaree Valley, 2013.

We became friendly with a younger generation of people who worked at the Normaway, especially Brooks Hart and Sean Murphy. Sean's grandfather owned a farm on a large hill overlooking the Normaway Inn, and Rhoda and I became friendly with Sean and his family. Brooks Hart was the grandson of owners of a farm, Heart of Harts, located in Northeast Margaree. The farm had guests, and it catered to children, an arrangement that Rose Tompkins offered on a less formal basis. After Brooks inherited the home and farm, he considered reviving the business of farm vacations but instead decided to concentrate on teaching culinary arts at the University of Cape Breton in Port Hawksbury. He has promoted local businesses in the Margaree area and was the force behind the establishment of the breakfast and lunch place in Northeast Margaree, The Dancing Goat.

Rhoda and I enjoyed the work of a local artisan, Josef MacKinnon, who carved figures out of wood. I had him carve a figure of a fisherman and showed him Robert's picture to guide him in his efforts. I gave the finished product to Robert as a gift. I later bought a figure of Charles Darwin from MacKinnon which captures the essence of that great nineteenth century British naturalist. MacKinnon had a workshop/studio right off where Egypt Road ends at the Cabot Trail road leading to Baddeck. He and his family spent the majority of the year in their home in Baddeck.

We have maintained our friendship with Frances Hart over the years. She was in charge of the Salmon Museum in Northeast Margaree, running the museum from its inception in 1965 until 2019. By the time she retired to her cozy home in Margaree Centre, near where her cousins and other members of the extended Hart family live, she had become synonymous with the museum. In honor of her service to the museum, she was given a lifetime membership to the Margaree Salmon Association. Unhappily, I recently learned that Frances passed away on April 20, 2025. She was 95.

The people of Margaree epitomize why the time we spent in Cape Breton was so meaningful to my family and me. The fundamental decency of the people we met has made our summers there so worthwhile. It is not just the landscape, the scent of freshly gathered hay in the clean air, and the serenity of the place, but it has been the wonderful people we have been privileged to get to know that has made our experience so important in our lives.

[**Note:** Storch, Laila (2008). *Marcel Tabuteau: How Do You Expect to Play the Oboe If You Can't Peel a Mushroom?*. Bloomington: Indiana University Press.]

Afterword:
"Farewell to Nova Scotia"

The Tompkins farm, August 1948.

Farewell to Nova Scotia" is a popular folk song from the province. It was adapted from the 1781 Scottish lament, "The Soldier's Adieu," and popularized during World War I. It has been sung numerous times since then and is part of the repertoire of such artists as Gordon Lightfoot, the Irish Rovers, the High Kings, Stompin' Tom Connors, and many more. Some of the artists that performed in the living room of The Normaway Inn used to sing the song, and it had great meaning for me in later years. I reflected over the fact that our boys were grown, and Rhoda and I might not get the opportunity to travel to Margaree again.

This had increased impact on me when Rhoda became ill. We did get to go to Margaree in 2019, just before the COVID pandemic took hold. Rhoda was happy that she could visit, and traveling there gave her great joy. I knew that this would probably be the last time we would be able to go together to Cape Breton—and it was.

Noticeable changes were occurring to the Cape Breton I had known for many years. In 2018, Mike Tompkins's more than a century-old farmhouse was taken down. The Tompkins extended family decided that because their relatives were scattered and the house needed extensive work, it was not worth making the necessary repairs to the home, and thus it was not practical to maintain it any longer.

Years before, in early 1976, Rose's nephew, Alec Miller, tore down Rose's home, the place I had stayed with my parents and my sister, and where Rhoda and I had spent our honeymoon. He had also taken down Rose's barns and chicken coop a few years earlier. He built his retirement home on the plot of land where the barns had stood. He also built a big red barn slightly north of the property. All that is left of the original farm is Mike Tompkins's old-fashioned grayish-brown barn, a type that once familiarly dotted the Margaree landscape.

My memories of Cape Breton remain an indelible part of my life. My last glimpse of the Margaree Valley was in August of 2022, a year after Rhoda's passing. Mark, George, and I took our last look at the beautiful Margaree Valley, realizing that perhaps we might not be able to return again. But I will never forget the time I spent in Cape Breton, with Mom and Dad, Rhoda, and our sons, Mark and George, and Susan and Robert. The gentle beauty of Margaree and the people who live here make this place special. I will never forget any of this.

"Farewell to Nova Scotia" (Chorus)

Farewell to Nova Scotia, the sea bound coast.
Let your mountains dark dreary be
For when I am far away on the briny ocean
tossed
Will you ever heave a sigh or wish for me?

Rose and Mike Tompkins Farm, Margaree Ford,
early 2000s.

Cap Rouge in Cape Breton Highlands National Park,
looking northwards, early 2000s.

Acknowledgements

Publication of this book has not been the work of one individual but the product of many who were extremely helpful along the way. They deserve to be mentioned for their support. A former classmate of mine at the University of Rochester as well as a friend, Susan Klein, professor emeritus at Indiana University, recommended that I should contact Thea Rademacher, president of Flint Hills Publishing, to see if there would be interest in my book about a special place in a corner of Nova Scotia, Canada, Cape Breton Island. This was fortuitous, because it led to a very productive working relationship. The time I have worked with Thea has been a real joy. She, in turn, directed me to Tabitha Ellwood, who has made many useful editorial suggestions during the last stages of publication, and has provided a great deal of insight in strengthening the work.

Members of a writing group I have been a part of for more than ten years, composed of fellow retired professors at City University of New York, have been very supportive with their advice and encouragement in helping my efforts to turn the bits and pieces about a very special place into the finished product: Professors Constance H. Gemson, the leader of our group and Irvin Sam Schonfeld, and David Kotelchuk, were very helpful in shaping this work.

The people of Cape Breton played an indirect but important role in developing this narrative. They made my family's travels to Nova Scotia such a rewarding adventure. Many have been cited in the book, and other individuals who my family and I have had brief contact with but are not cited, nevertheless have made our experience there so worthwhile.

I am continually indebted to my late parents and my wife, Rhoda, who are an integral part of this story, and who made it possible for me to discover and rediscover this magical part of the world. My sister, Susan, and her husband, Dr. Robert Davidson, played an important role in sharing this story. Lastly, my sons, Mark and George, have provided invaluable assistance in many aspects of this work, supplying photographs, technical assistance, as well as being a steady source of strength for me.

About the Author

Joel S. Schwartz is Professor Emeritus of Biology at the City University of New York, College of Staten Island, where he taught for forty years. His scholarly interest has been in the history of biology, focused on nineteenth-century natural history, on the development of the theory of evolution, and how maritime exploration stimulated discovery in the natural sciences. He is the author of two books in the field, *Darwin's Disciple: George John Romanes, A Life in Letters*, and *Robert Brown and Mungo Park: Travels and Explorations in Natural History for the Royal Society*. In addition, he has written numerous scholarly articles in the history of biology. He and his family have traveled extensively in North America and Europe, and he spent considerable time at Cambridge University and London, studying the papers of Charles Darwin and other naturalists.

www.flinthillspublishing.com/joel-schwartz

www.ingramcontent.com/pod-product-compliance
Lightning Source LLC
Chambersburg PA
CBHW040845120626
46547CB00001B/33